great inventions

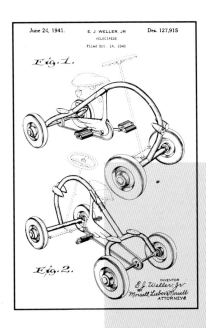

June 24, 1941. E. J. WELLER, JR Des. 127,915
VELOCIPEDE
Filed Oct. 14, 1940

Fig. 1.

Fig. 2.

INVENTOR
E.J. Weller, Jr
Morsell Luber Morsell
ATTORNEYS

good intentions

great inventions

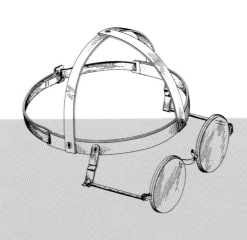

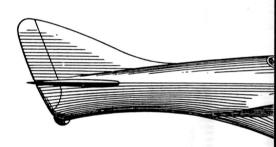

good intentions

United States

GREAT INVENTIONS • GOOD INTENTIONS

Patent Office

CHRONICLE BOOKS • SAN FRANCISCO **ERIC BAKER** TEXT BY JANE MARTIN

¶ Library of Congress Cataloging-in-Publication Data: Baker, Eric, 1949- ¶ Great inventions, good intentions: an illustrated history of American design patents / by Eric Baker; text by Jane Martin. ¶ p. cm. ¶ Includes bibliographical references. ¶ ISBN 0-87701-760-3 ¶ 1. Design Protection—United States. ¶ I. Martin, Jane R. II. Title. ¶ TS171.4.B34 1990 ¶ 608.73—dc20 ¶ 90-33690 CIP

Book and cover design: Eric Baker, Chip Kidd.

Distributed in Canada by Raincoast Books   112 East Third Avenue, Vancouver, B.C. V5T 1C8

10 9 8 7 6 5 4 3 2 1

Chronicle Books ¶ 275 Fifth Street ¶ San Francisco, California 94103

Design patent drawing on page 2: Combined Goggles and Support Therefore ¶ November 11, 1941 ¶ Percival C. Monjar ¶ 130,310.

For permission to reprint from the writings of Henry Dreyfuss we thank Henry Dreyfuss Associates, which he founded in 1929. The firm still provides industrial design and human factors consulting to some of the nation's better known companies. ¶ Excerpt on page 35 reprinted by permission of Putnam Publishing Group, from *We* by Charles Lindbergh, © 1927 by G.P. Putnam's Sons. ¶ Radio schedule on page 100 and Depression price list on page 137 from *This Fabulous Century: 1930-1940*, by the editors of Time-Life Books, © 1969 Time-Life Books, Inc. ¶ Excerpts on pages 71 and 124 reprinted from *Home Mechanix* magazine, © 1934-6 by Times Mirror Magazines.

This project was supported in part by a grant from the National Endowment for the Arts, a Federal Agency.

In our research in the Patent Archives in New York City and Washington, D.C., we came across far more design patents than could fit on these pages. Narrowing down the selection was a difficult task, for these drawings are seldom seen and deserve exposure.

This book is one of ideas more than products, of the inventor's solitary pursuit of the American dream as well as the professional designer's response to a corporate assignment. It's a combination of detective work and hundreds of hours of personal research. *Great Inventions, Good Intentions* is essentially a personal archive, and, though the designs included will speak of different things to different viewpoints, it is our hope that it will be enjoyed by all. It is also our hope that it will serve as a guidepost to the hidden treasures available for anyone who would take the time to discover them.

This book has been a combined effort of many individuals who shared our enthusiasm and belief in the material. Special thanks go to Tyler Blik, Kenneth Kneitel, Chip Kidd, Patrick Seymour, Susanna Oberhelman, John Baeder, Richard Merkin, Dorothy Globus, Seymour Chwast, Paula Scher, Tom Bonauro, Steven Heller, Karen Minster, Fearn Cutler, David Barich, Lisa Howard and Annie Barrows of Chronicle Books, Peter Miller, Emily Schaab, and Myrna and Nancy Martin. Very special thanks to Bonnie Resnick and Nathaniel Knight for their encouragement and support and to Harold Martin for his memories and expertise. At the United States Patent and Trademark Office, gratitude goes to Kenneth Cage, former Director, Special Laws Administration and Director of Designs, and Wallace R. Burke, Supervisory Patent Examiner, provided us with invaluable information during interviews, and to Oscar Mastin, Director of Public Affairs.

Dedicated to all the famous and not-so-famous designers and inventors whose ideas are an inspiration to us all.

contents

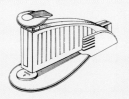

The cavernous front room at the New York Public Library's Research Annex is full of readers huddled over ancient tomes, sitting at broad tables that have clearly seen better days. The microfilm terminals whir and click, the fluorescent lights flicker and buzz. Through a nondescript doorway is another room with more tables. Here, among the patent holdings, there's a different buzz in the air. ¶ Inventors use this room as a home away from home, sitting for hours in the same chair, poring over Official Gazettes. The patent lawyers they hire—to make sure their patent is actually new, to fill out paperwork, to keep abreast of the laws, and quite possibly to gather evidence in an infringement suit—come and go with a slightly better-dressed ease. Becoming familiar with the vast holdings can take years, for the room is a warehouse of ideas—a mother-lode of gazettes and journals, shelved on stacks that extend far back into the room, though they're hidden from view by a glass and cinderblock wall that's painted, like everything else, easy-eye green. ¶ Research for a previous book on trademarks uncovered a fascinating distraction in the old Official Gazettes, which contain the patented industrial designs of the masters—Henry Dreyfuss, Walter Dorwin Teague, Norman Bel Geddes—in two-dimensional form. There are also drawings for designs done on a different kind of assignment, by independent inventors who may never have gotten a company contract in their lives. Sadie O'Neil's flamenco dancer restaurant and S. J. Hudson's dirigible ashtray were meticulously rendered by professional draftspeople who were well acquainted with the U.S. Patent Office's stringent requirements. No matter what a design is for or whether or not it will ever be manufactured, its patent drawing is treated—by law—with bureaucratic solemnity. ¶ The first patent law was enacted in 1790 to "promote the progress of science and useful arts" by granting patents as temporary deeds of property. In 1842 the Patent Office—then in the State Department—made the designs themselves patentable

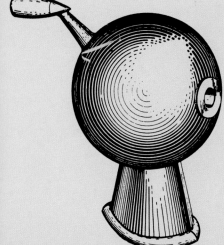

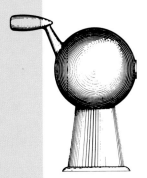

(the first one issued was for a typeface). In addition to the drawing, a model of the invention was required for both design and utility patents (the former protects external appearance, the latter internal workings). Soon the models covered innumerable feet of government shelf space. By 1880, when the model requirement was rescinded, maintaining the models had become a costly, full-time enterprise. Drawings would have to do. ¶ The many tiers of the patent system start long before a patent is granted. An application first prompts a search, then a response, then countless revisions. Even in the 1930s, when a country scrambling to get out of the Depression hailed technology as its saving grace, patent examiners were faced with a bureaucracy which had matured during the 19th century. There were 62 categories for classifying inventions—from machine parts to bud vases—and the search through prior patents to confirm an invention's originality might include any number of them. Though a 1952 law redirected examiners to first consider inventions of similar function, a search could still lead almost anywhere. A shoe could feature a buckle

which was once patented on its own. A car could include a door handle once patented for a refrigerator. A lampshade might imitate the patented design for a hat. For this reason, design patents depend primarily on the strength of the drawing submitted in the application. ¶ Utility patents use drawings to show examples of the mechanical scheme and may also contain copious pages of text, but a design patent uses the drawing as its main claim and the paperwork is minimal. A person "skilled in the art," as patent language goes, should be able to reproduce the housing and ornamentation described directly from the drawing. Strict rules govern everything from shading ("oblique parallel lines spaced sufficiently apart") to light source (from the "upper left-hand corner at an angle of 45 degrees"). The law's explicit instructions ensure that a design patent drawing will be endowed with an explicit character that its three-dimensional incarnation, if there is one, won't have. ¶ Many of the design patents

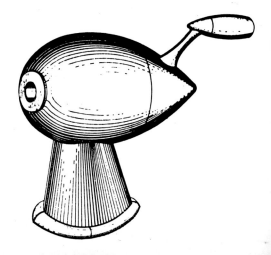

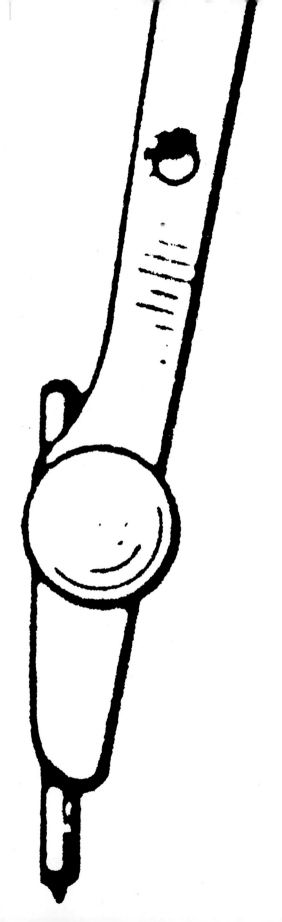

in this book were never manufactured. Unlike the highly commercial function of patenting today, where a patent is often a formality protecting a product which has already been produced (inventors have a year to file), patenting in the heady years of the Depression and World War II was an act of great faith. "Invent, invent!" exhorted *Modern Mechanix* magazine to its readers in 1935, not only because they might strike it rich, but because their invention might benefit the country. During the war years spent protecting "freedom," the freedom to invent was one worth practicing again and again. ¶ The design patents in this book which were manufactured include the first incarnations of classics: the Scotch tape dispenser, Schwinn's bicycle, and aviator sunglasses. Their shapes have a rhyme and reason that reflect their times. Scientific breakthroughs such as the wind-tunnel, sheet-metal, and plastics opened up frontiers of speed and created new methods of manufacturing. Accounts, however fictional, of outer space, on radio programs like

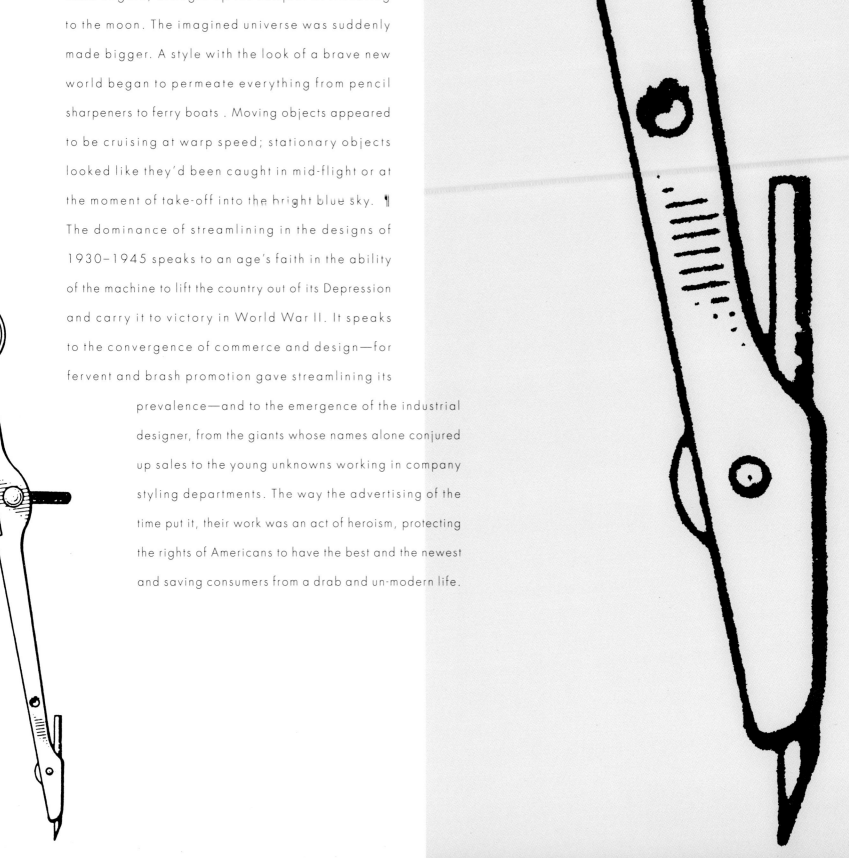

Buck Rogers, brought up the subject of traveling to the moon. The imagined universe was suddenly made bigger. A style with the look of a brave new world began to permeate everything from pencil sharpeners to ferry boats . Moving objects appeared to be cruising at warp speed; stationary objects looked like they'd been caught in mid-flight or at the moment of take-off into the bright blue sky. ¶ The dominance of streamlining in the designs of 1930–1945 speaks to an age's faith in the ability of the machine to lift the country out of its Depression and carry it to victory in World War II. It speaks to the convergence of commerce and design—for fervent and brash promotion gave streamlining its prevalence—and to the emergence of the industrial designer, from the giants whose names alone conjured up sales to the young unknowns working in company styling departments. The way the advertising of the time put it, their work was an act of heroism, protecting the rights of Americans to have the best and the newest and saving consumers from a drab and un-modern life.

Nothing symbolized machine-age progress like a car, speeding with aerodynamic power down a brand-new road. The automobile industry, stunned by the Crash of 1929, found their survival strategy in design. Led by General Motors' head of styling, Harley Earl, car companies began to employ designers to give their models a desirably modern appeal. By the early '30s even Henry Ford conceded that packaging, not engineering, clinched a sale. The institution of the annual model change had begun.
¶ But the imagination of the public wasn't just fueled by the sturdy examples of streamlining presented at the annual auto shows; nor was the inspiration of designers fueled by the edicts of Detroit executives. European discoveries in aerodynamics regularly transcended standards of speed, arriving at forms that offered less and less resistance to onrushing winds. In America Buckminster Fuller produced his 1934, three-wheeled Dymaxion car—a fuel-efficient, six-passenger teardrop; though only three were made, the car's design was influential. Norman Bel Geddes built models of streamlined vehicles that were fantastic masses of seamless, parabolic curves. ¶ The machine age had tremendous faith in the potential of the engine, and in the ability of automation to take innovations and adapt them, albeit gradually, for commercial production. Chrysler's commercially produced 1934 Airflow was a failure despite its streamlined profile—confirming Earl's belief that buying a car was a far more conservative act than looking at one. But two years later Lincoln's V-12 Zephyr and the fabulous Cord 810 swept the auto shows in storms of applause. Bel Geddes's talent for prophecy reached a zenith when he was hired by General Motors not to design a car,

transportation

but to design a world. His conception of transportation, circa 1960, for the 1939 New York World's Fair featured cloverleaf interchanges, freeways, and office towers. The exhibit, Futurama, was the star of Flushing Meadow Park, drawing 5 million viewers in one year. ¶ Technological improvements played many roles in design. Raymond Loewy took advantage of sheet-metal and welding techniques to fashion silver-skinned cruisers for Greyhound beginning in 1933, enabling the burgeoning long-distance bus industry to become a more attractive—and less expensive—alternative to train service. Until the '29 Crash the railroads had enjoyed a de facto

domination, but they too would find ways to improve their image without compromising their strengths. Loewy and Henry Dreyfuss designed streamlined steel shrouds to give bulky but powerful steam engines a sleeker, faster look. Recently developed diesel engines fascinated the American public with their all-aluminum, lightweight cars, which were hailed as the future of railroading embodied in the present. To keep sight of what he considered the true future, Bel Geddes continued to lead the vanguard with racy bullet-trains. Though never produced they had a lasting influence on the shape of trains to come. ¶ Ironically, the future of railroading was influenced less by bullet-trains than by flying machines. With air travel still daring and expensive in the

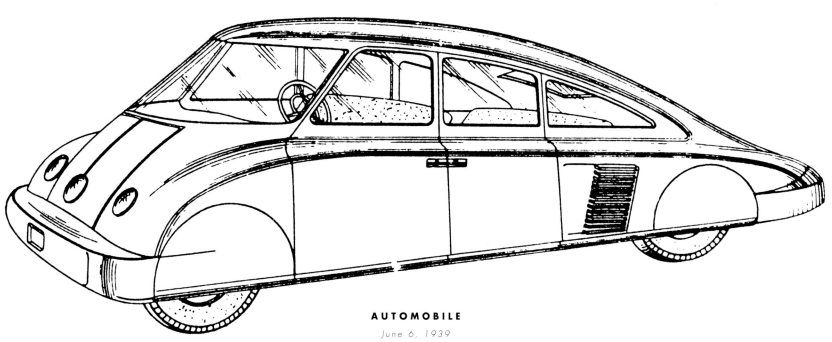

AUTOMOBILE
June 6, 1939
Walter D. Teague Walter D. Teague, Jr.
115,177

30s but clearly full of potential, railroading's dominance would soon end. Developments in stressed aluminum, better engines, and aeronautic principles improved the design of both land and water-based planes, though without viable landing strips or well-charted courses, water-based planes were considered safer. Giant flying boats that could take off from and land on the water brought a practical glamour to aviation, carrying more fuel and holding more passengers in their splendid cabins that the biggest land planes of the day. But land planes were by no means primitive. The integrated, monocoque design of the Douglas DC-1, which was introduced in 1933, heralded a revolution. Gone were the heavily braced wings and boxy fuselages, the awkward rivet patterns, the wicker chairs bolted to the floor. Here was a plane dedicated to passenger flight which would improve steadily with each successive model. The DC-3 demonstrated phenomenal toughness under the worst conditions of the war. ¶ The war effort pushed air travel to take quantum leaps. But in the 1930s flight was a wide open field of unanswered questions—about distance, stability, power, and materials—that prompted great and fearless experimentation. What is now regarded as an amusing flop might then have seemed full of promise. Howard Hughes's colossal flying boat flew a total of a mile on twelve engines. John Northrop's great flying wing wouldn't get off the ground for decades except into the skies of comic books and radio. Inventors patented personal helicopter designs and car-boat-planes whose wings folded like an insect's. Nautical designs contained their own responses, borrowing liberally from the designs of cars and planes. Loewy created boats that were slimmer and longer than ever before. Even accessories seemed imbued with a streamlined power. The mystique of motion was powerful, and it blurred the boundaries between land, water, and sea.

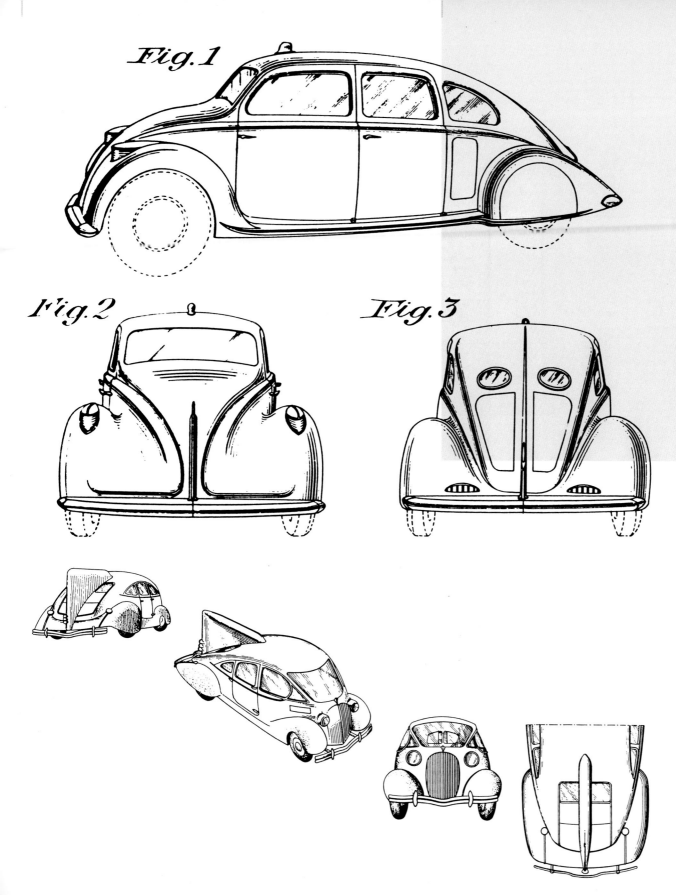

AUTOMOBILE
January 22, 1935
John Tjaarda
94,396

John Tjaarda's streamlined "Automobile" (Des. 94,396) is one of many cars the Dutch-born stylist designed in his quest for the ideal: an inexpensively produced union of body and frame. His early conceptions, with their rear engines and divided rear windows, may have influenced the Volkswagen Beetle. Later work done on the job at Briggs Manufacturing—the largest supplier of auto bodies for both Ford and Chrysler— caught the attention of Edsel Ford, who was looking for a new design for Lincoln. Ford commissioned Tjaarda to work secretly on what would be a stellar expression of Tjaarda's aerodynamic training. It made its first appearance at Chicago's 1934 Century of Progress Exposition as Brigg's Dream Car. Revised under Edsel Ford's sure guidance—its front end was sharpened into a pointed grille and its engine was moved to the front—it became the influential Lincoln Zephyr V-12 of 1936, called by the Museum of Modern Art "the first successfully streamlined car in America."

AUTOMOBILE
March 23, 1937
C. Charles Walker
103,772

Streamlining's stylistic milestones include Norman Bel Geddes's Motor Car Number 9 (Des. 93,863), a wonder of aerodynamics shaped by its inventor's belief in the rear-engine, teardrop form. The car was the essence of motion, a radical, futuristic fantasy far exceeding the bounds of conventional manufacturing. Like most of Bel Geddes's conceptions it was never produced, but helped to make streamlining popular.

Gordon Buehrig's brilliant design for the Cord 810 (Des. 93,451), a front-wheel-drive speed machine, featured teardrop fenders, a long tapering hood, and a horizontally lined grill with chrome exhaust pipes (installed later) that clearly alluded to the powerful V-8 engine inside. It captured the 1936 auto shows; despite the high price of $3,000 hundreds of orders poured in for this perfect embodiment of the latest in automotive design. But the rush to finish hand-made (and undrivable) prototypes for the auto shows had preempted getting the Cord's kinks out, particularly in its feisty front end. In two years of production only 2,320 were built.

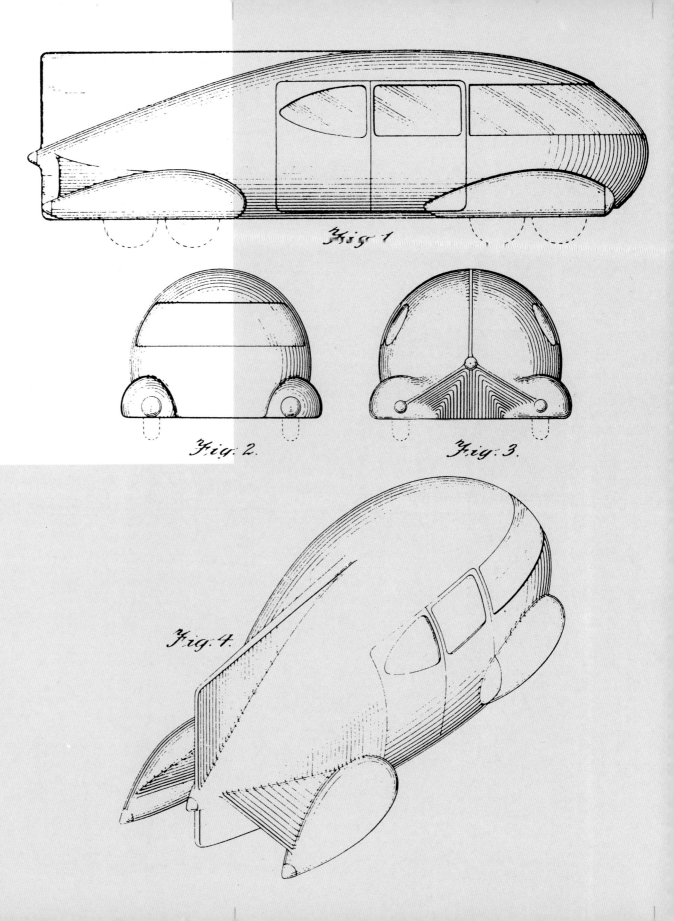

Fig. 1.

Fig. 2.

Fig. 3.

Fig. 4.

AUTOMOTIVE VEHICLE
November 20, 1934
Norman Bel Geddes
William H. Stangle
Worthen Paxton
93,863

Within a few years, cars lost some of their more baroque features such as running boards and massive pontoon fenders, though they were still streamlined. Chrysler stylist Ralph Roberts patented the bulbous design of the Thunderbolt (Des. 129,618) in 1941—one of two Chrysler show cars that combined traditional styling with flowing, sheet-metal forms. Designed to rival the extravagant dream cars produced in small numbers by General Motors, the Thunderbolt had push-button controls for its windows, door locks, retractable top, and headlights. Speed was now implied with a tapering "whisker" that wrapped around the lower hood to the front end. Roberts's design lent a number of motifs and lines to Chrysler models throughout the 1940s and 1950s and served as a thematic prototype for the postwar Packard.

AUTOMOBILE
September 23, 1941
Ralph S. Roberts
129,618

AUTOMOBILE

June 23, 1931

Alan H. Leamy

84,484

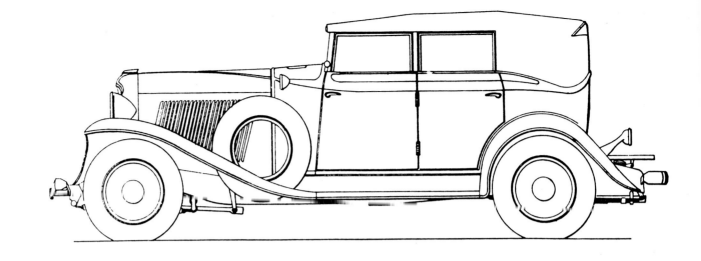

AUTOMOBILE

February 3, 1931

Raymond Loewy

83,205

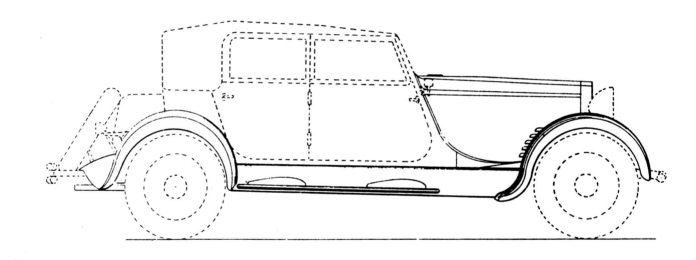

AUTOMOBILE

April 16, 1935

G. Grummer

G. Busson

95,247

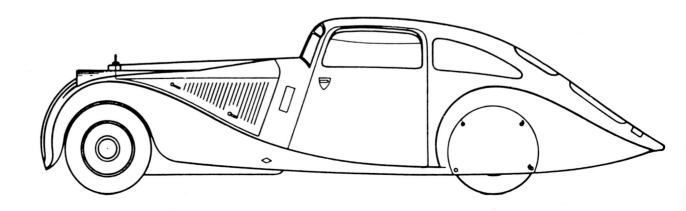

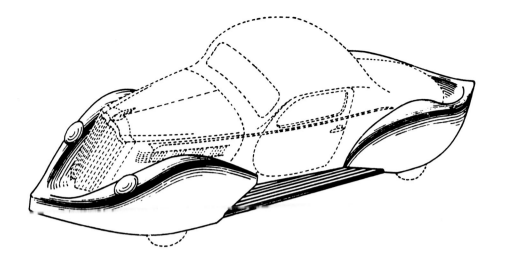

AUTOMOTIVE VEHICLE
May 2, 1939
Thomas F. King
114,579

AUTOMOBILE
January 19, 1937
Douglas Frederick Harold Fitzmaurice
102,852

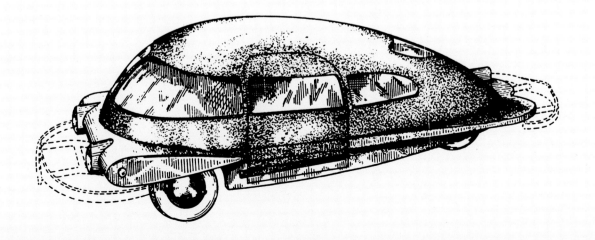

AUTOMOBILE
November 14, 1939
Paul M. Lewis
117,636

CAB-OVER-ENGINE FUEL
TANK TRUCK

August 31, 1937

Alexis de Sakhnoffsky

105,899

GASOLINE TANK VEHICLE

February 1, 1938

Alexis de Sakhnoffsky

108,269

TANK VEHICLE

March 30, 1937

Ralph L. Kuss

103,821

 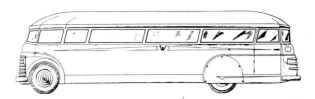

VEHICLE

October 6, 1936

Alexis de Sakhnoffsky

101,507

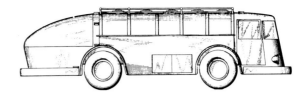 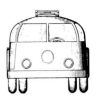

**MOTOR DRIVEN TANK
TRUCK**

April 18, 1933

Howard W. Kizer

89,642

MOTOR VEHICLE

April 26, 1932

Henry Tyler

86,871

VEHICLE

May 25, 1937

Oscar F. Jackson

104,688

TANK TRUCK

January 4, 1938

Edward H. Gill

107,770

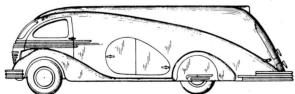

 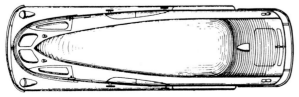

TANK VEHICLE

September 29, 1936

John F. Frazier

101,350

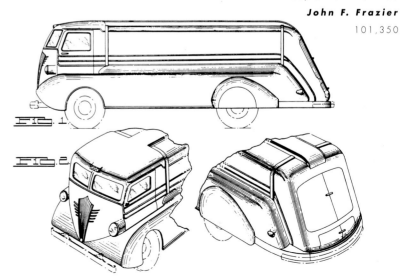

AUTOMOBILE RADIATOR
CAP ORNAMENT

November 17, 1936

Albert Sebek

102,007

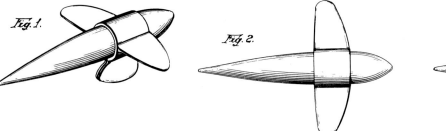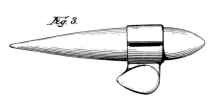

RADIATOR CAP
ORNAMENT

June 23, 1931

William B. Vandegrift

Sigfred O. Bystrom

84,502

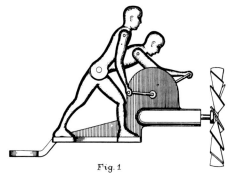

Fig. 1   Fig. 2

AUTOMOBILE RADIATOR
ORNAMENT

January 7, 1936

Franklin Q. Hershey

98,068

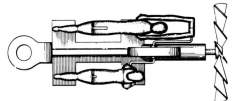

AUTOMOBILE ORNAMENT

July 21, 1936

Herbert V. Henderson

100,497

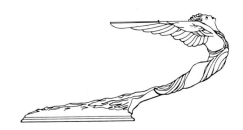

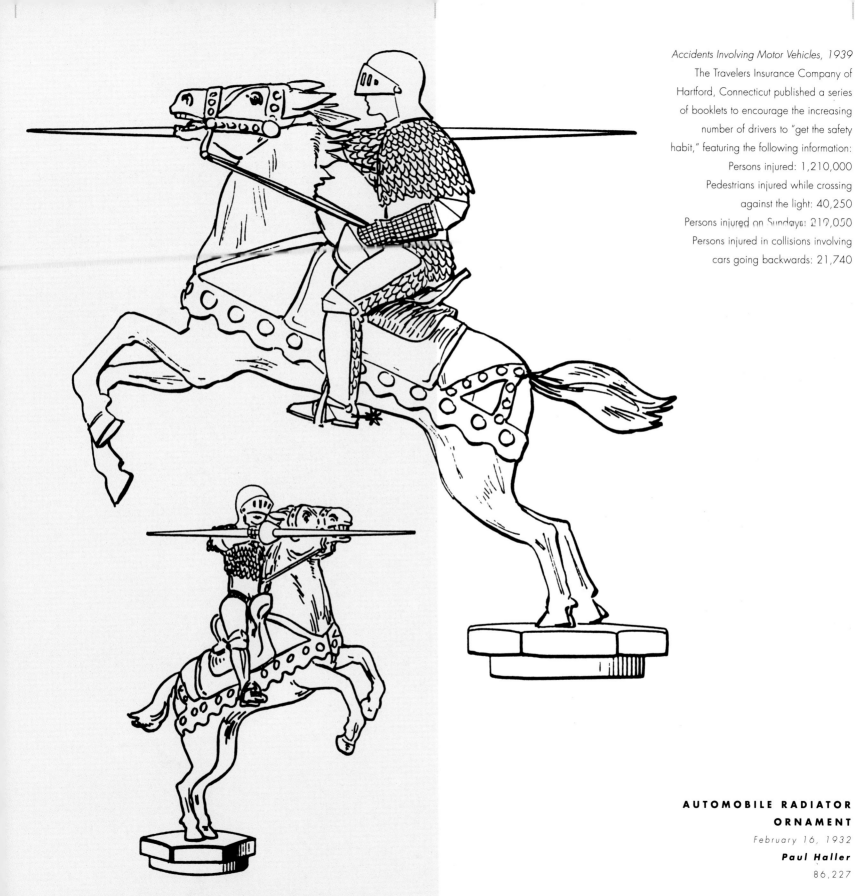

Accidents Involving Motor Vehicles, 1939
The Travelers Insurance Company of
Hartford, Connecticut published a series
of booklets to encourage the increasing
number of drivers to "get the safety
habit," featuring the following information:
Persons injured: 1,210,000
Pedestrians injured while crossing
against the light: 40,250
Persons injured on Sundays: 212,050
Persons injured in collisions involving
cars going backwards: 21,740

**AUTOMOBILE RADIATOR
ORNAMENT**
February 16, 1932
Paul Haller
86,227

TRAILER OR SIMILAR ARTICLE

September 29, 1936

Estok Menton

101,384

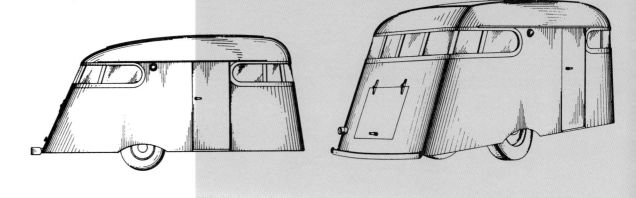

AUTOMOBILE TRAILER BODY

November 3, 1936

Alexis de Sakhnoffsky

101,809

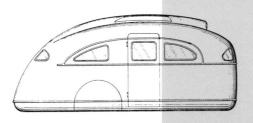
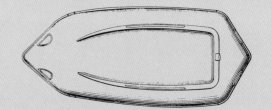

AUTOMOBILE TRAILER BODY

August 4, 1936

Ace. H. Alexander

100,679

TRAILER

February 18, 1936

Fred E. Kaunitz

Lester R. Kaunitz

98,650

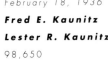

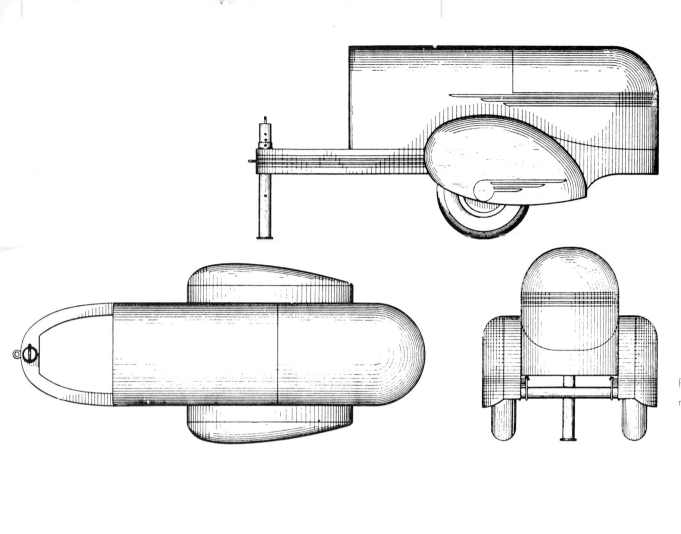

PORTABLE HEATER
January 9, 1940
Clifford Brooks Stevens
188,514

In the early years of nomadic vacationing, trailers symbolized not only freedom, but also the progress in design and science that had brought that freedom about. Trailers were designed to match the pontoon fenders of streamlined cars, to resemble modern houses or space-age containers of sleek aluminum. Custom automobile body builder and industrial designer Alexis de Sakhnoffsky patented a utility trailer (Des. 101,809) that looked like the back half of a car. John R. Morgan, who had worked as an industrial designer for Sears before returning to private practice in 1935, drafted an elegant vacation trailer (Des. 105,073) that combined subtly advanced details with popular appeal.

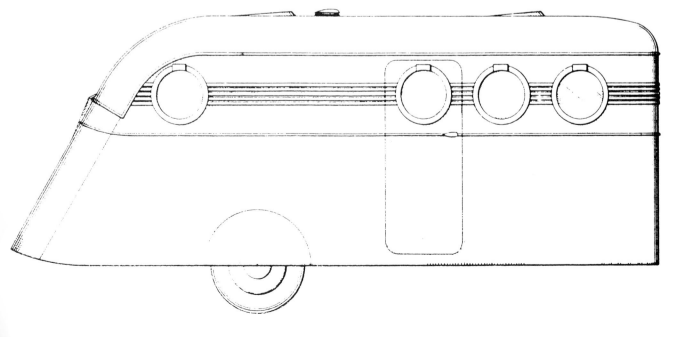

TRAILER
June 22, 1937
John R. Morgan
105,073

**HOUSING FOR
DISPENSING APPARATUS**

June 6, 1939

Hosmer L. Blum

115,143

**GASOLINE DISPENSING
UNIT**

March 29, 1932

T.L. Pflueger

80,033

**HOUSING FOR
DISPENSING APPARATUS**

October 27, 1936

William M. Hutchison

101,739

**GASOLINE DISPENSING
PUMP**

February 2, 1932

Earl E. Eickmeyer

Harley H. Wolfe

86,115

**LIQUID DISPENSING
APPARATUS**

April 7, 1936

William M. Griffin

99,193

**FLUID DISPENSING
APPARATUS**

April 19, 1932

William M. Griffin

86,770

**FLUID DISPENSING
APPARATUS**

May 10, 1932

Jacob W. Hartman, Jr.

86,915

**FLUID DISPENSING
APPARATUS**

May 17, 1932

William M. Griffin

86,954

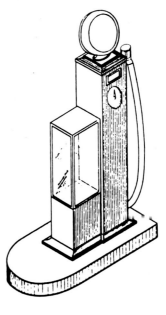
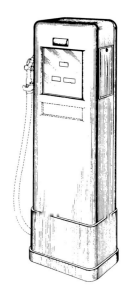
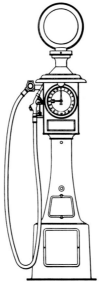
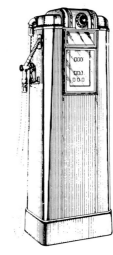

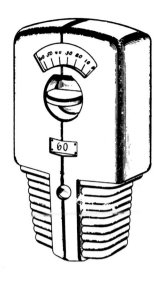
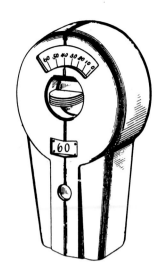
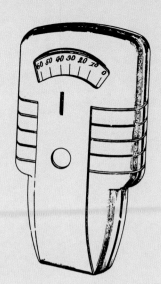

**PARKING METER
HOUSING**
December 21, 1937
Raymond Loewy
107,527, 107,529, 107,531

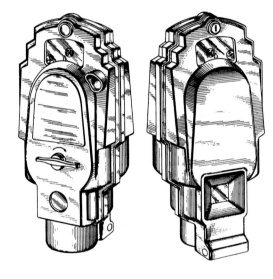
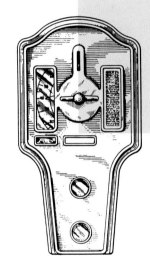

PARKING METER
September 1, 1936
David C. Rockola
101,067, 101,068

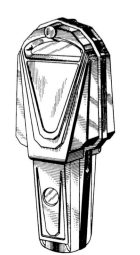

**PARKING METER
HOUSING**
December 21, 1937
John B. McGay
George E. Nicholson
107,577

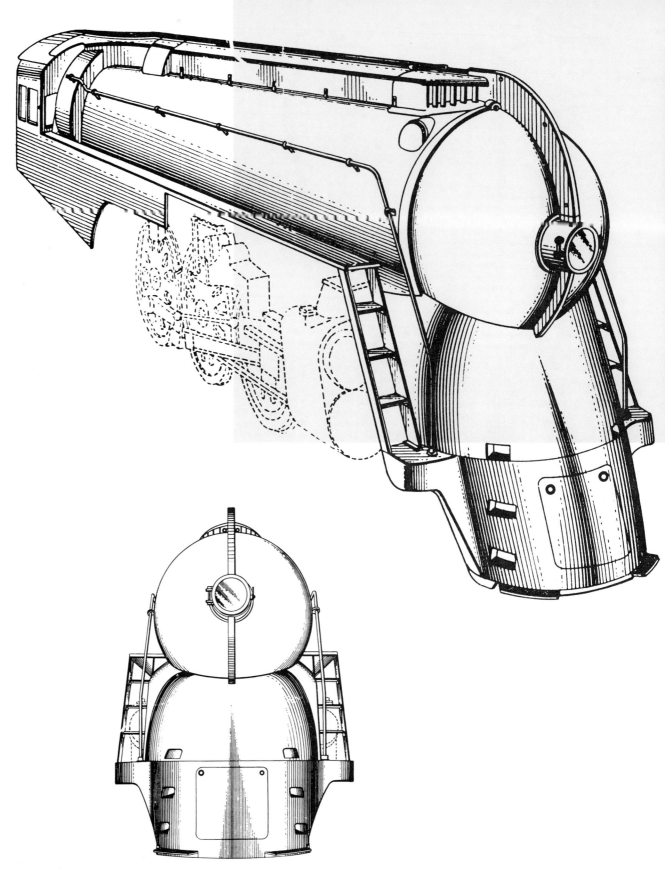

"One morning during the initial run of the [redesigned] 20th Century Limited there was a knock on my compartment door . . . it was a large maid, who asked, 'Are you Mr. Dreyfuss, who designed this train?' She continued, 'Did you design this uniform?' I said our office had supervised it, and asked what was wrong with it. She said scornfully, 'It looks Mammy-made.' When we got to Chicago I took her to Marshall Field's and bought her a uniform she thought was more appropriate to the new train— 'something in gray moire with a zipper.'"
—*Henry Dreyfuss*, Designing for People

Henry Dreyfuss received a commission from New York Central to design its 20th Century Limited, a first-class, all-pullman-car train that would take its passengers in high style on the prestigious New York–Chicago run. Dreyfuss designed a streamlined shroud (Des. 116,180) to cover the train's conventional Hudson-type locomotive, a 4-6-4 that devoured long distances at top speed. The 1938 redesigned 20th Century Limited made the New York–Chicago run with style in a record 16 hours. A mohawk-like blade along the engine's tapered front sliced the wind as the train raced along. Inside, passengers sat comfortably in their berths, compartments, and drawing rooms, enjoying, as Dreyfuss described, "The quiet luxury of a private club; your membership, a transportation ticket."

LOCOMOTIVE
August 15, 1939
Henry Dreyfuss
116,180

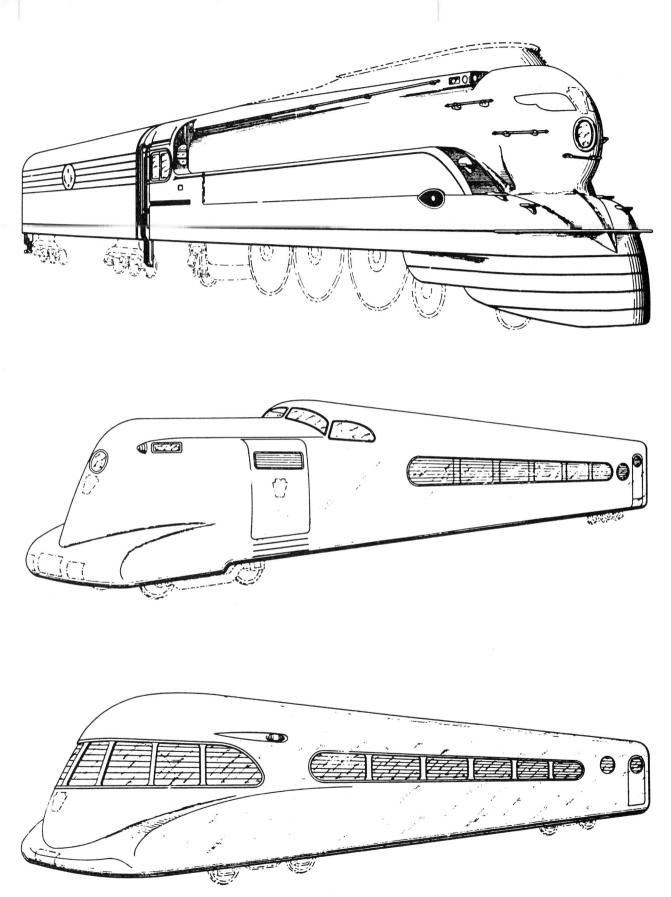

LOCOMOTIVE
September 21, 1937
Raymond Loewy
106,143

Competing for the New York–Chicago run was Pennsylvania Railroad's Broadway Limited, redesigned by Raymond Loewy. His version of a streamlined shroud for their 1938 S-1 locomotive drew heavily from his previous design for PRR's 1936 K4S. Its speedy form was improved in a series of patents (Des. 106,143). The flush headlight of the K4S was replaced by a projecting headlight in the S-1, and the chromium speed stripes that ran along the K4S's graduated cowl were extended to fluid lines along the S-1's sides. Both trains were long, duplex powerhouses (the S-1 covered 140 feet), but the S-1, inaugurated on the same day as Dreyfuss's new 20th Century, was hailed as the most elegant, daring, and powerful-looking train of its day.

Dreyfuss and Loewy agreed that a locomotive's power shouldn't be disguised. But Loewy's infatuation with the look of pure speed resulted in other highly advanced designs, particularly for self-contained or paired railway cars used on commuter runs (Des. 105,533 and 105,534). Many never saw service, but stretched the imagination of his client.

RAILWAY CAR UNIT
August 3, 1937
Raymond Loewy
Warren R. Elsey
105,533, 105,534

ARTICULATED RAIL CAR OR SIMILAR ARTICLE

June 16, 1936

Everett Eugene Adams
Martin P. Blomberg
William H. Mussey
William B. Stout

100,000

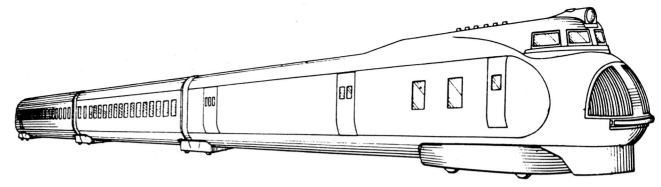

Pullman-Standard manufactured the first streamlined diesel train, the M-10000 (Des. 100,000) for Union-Pacific in 1934, and the unit of three articulated, air-conditioned cars with shared sets of wheels toured the country as the City of Salina. Without the extra wheels the engine pulled less weight, and air flowed past the bulldog snout and over the cars in a solid, uninterrupted stream. Echoing a futuristic, never-manufactured design by Norman Bel Geddes, the diesel train heralded a new efficiency in short-distance rail travel. At Pennsylvania Station, a proud Union Pacific distributed tiny aluminum coins to remind the public of the M-10000's new aluminum construction.

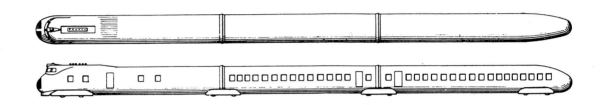

As diesel engines increased in power, Electro-Motive, a subsidiary of General Motors, arrived at a design for a diesel locomotive (Des. 129,410) that would become the standard engine type of the 1940s. Separating diesel engines from cars enabled diesel to take over as a mode of power, and as early as 1935, Electro-Motive manufactured separate diesels to replace steam engines on conventional trains.

LOCOMOTIVE BODY

September 9, 1941

Harold L. Hamilton
William D. Otter
Paul A. Meyer

129,410

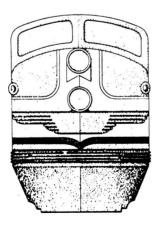

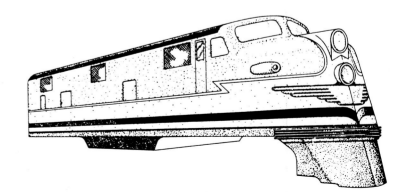

MOTOR COACH
January 24, 1939
Raymond Loewy
113,009

Greyhound's Orville Caesar commissioned Raymond Loewy to embark on a modernization campaign in 1933. The shape of buses had already evolved away from cab fronts, unwieldy roof racks, and observation platforms, but still had a stiff, boxy shape. Loewy streamlined corners from nose to window to taillight and drafted a series of racy trims (Des. 113,009; 129,411; 129,396; and 127,174) including a parabolic swoop over the front wheel. With his characteristic knack for creating designs to last, Loewy trimmed the Greyhound logo from a "fat mongrel" to a purebred in racing trim, and opted for an unpainted silver finish on the body of the bus. Working in an old power-boat showroom on Park Avenue, Loewy also built a double-decker prototype that would become Greyhound's first Scenicruiser right after the war.

MOTOR COACH
September 9, 1941
Raymond Loewy
129,411, 129,396

MOTOR COACH
May 13, 1941
Raymond Loewy
127,174

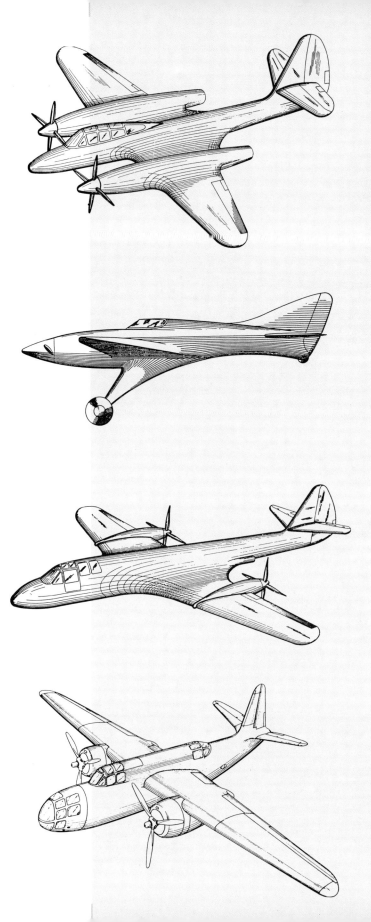

PURSUIT AIRPLANE

November 24, 1942

James S. McDonnell, Jr.

134,426

AIRPLANE

May 31, 1938

John Pavlecka

109,951

PURSUIT AIRPLANE

November 24, 1942

James S. McDonnell, Jr.

134,425

**ATTACK BOMBER
AIRPLANE**

July 1, 1941

**Edward H. Heinemann
Ernest J. Englebert**

128,027

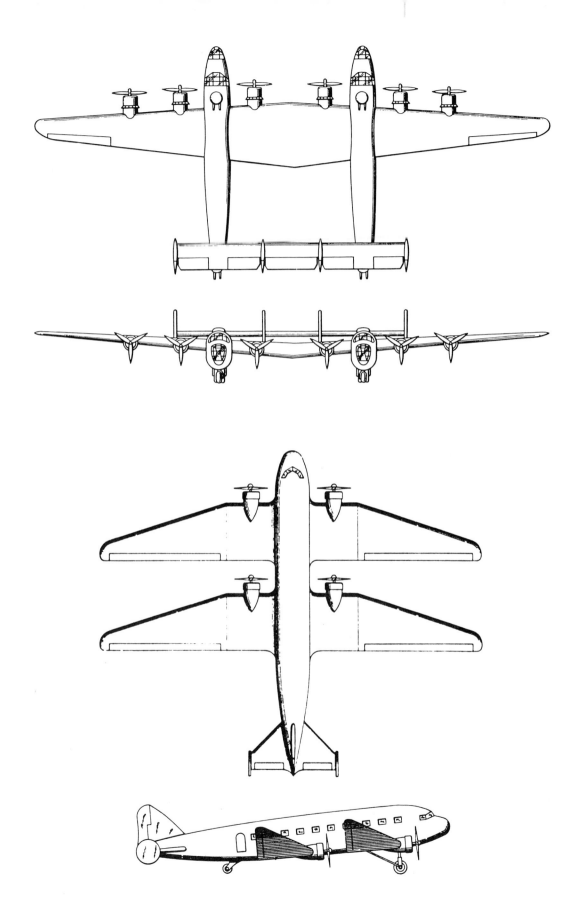

AIRPLANE
June 13, 1944
Allen O. Kelly
138,102

"Trans-Atlantic service is still in the future. Extensive research and careful study will be required before any regular schedule between America and Europe can be maintained. Multi-motored flying boats with stations along the route will eventually make trans-oceanic airlines practical but their development must be based on a solid foundation of experience and equipment."
—*Charles Lindbergh, We*

**TANDEM WING
MONOPLANE**
May 13, 1941
L.E. Oliver
127,159

TRANSOCEANIC FLYING BOAT

February 27, 1934

Lessiter C. Milburn

91,634

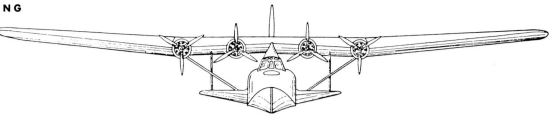

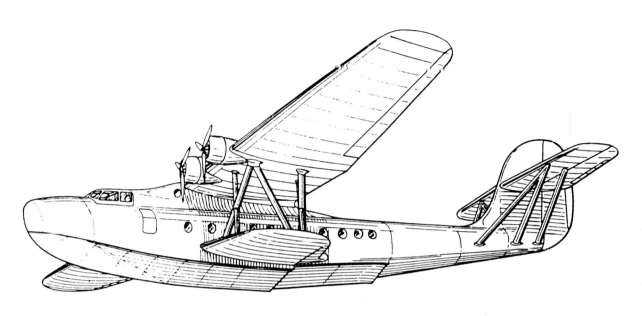

AIRPLANE

January 30, 1934

Thomas. M. Shelton

91,444

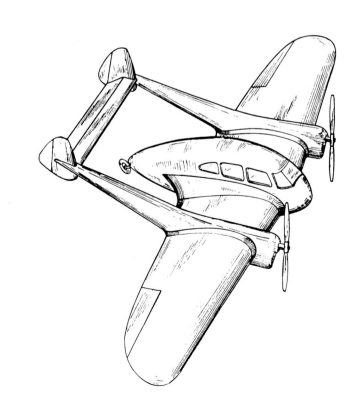

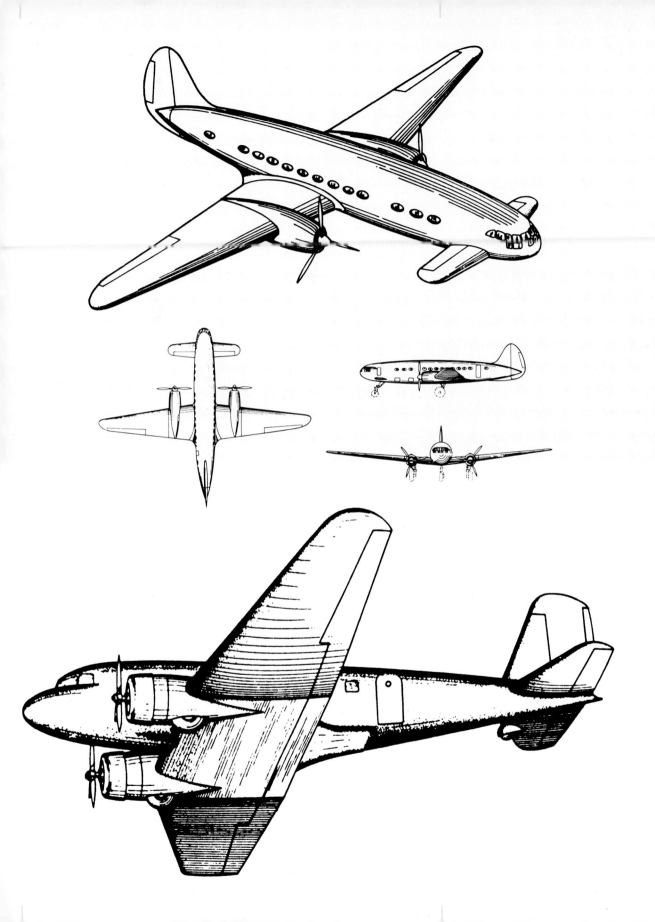

AIRPLANE
August 8, 1939
Clarence L. Johnson
116, 094

AIRPLANE
January 29, 1935
James H. Kindelberger
Arthur E. Raymond
94,427

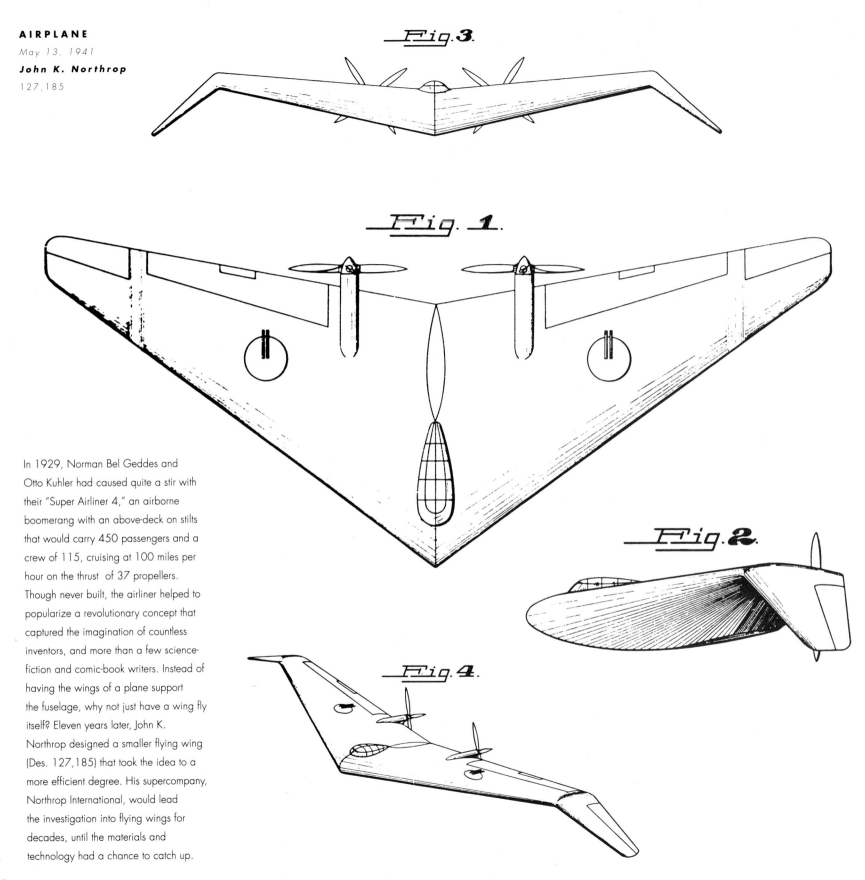

AIRPLANE

May 13, 1941

John K. Northrop

127,185

Fig.3.

Fig. 1.

Fig. 2.

Fig. 4.

In 1929, Norman Bel Geddes and Otto Kuhler had caused quite a stir with their "Super Airliner 4," an airborne boomerang with an above-deck on stilts that would carry 450 passengers and a crew of 115, cruising at 100 miles per hour on the thrust of 37 propellers. Though never built, the airliner helped to popularize a revolutionary concept that captured the imagination of countless inventors, and more than a few science-fiction and comic-book writers. Instead of having the wings of a plane support the fuselage, why not just have a wing fly itself? Eleven years later, John K. Northrop designed a smaller flying wing (Des. 127,185) that took the idea to a more efficient degree. His supercompany, Northrop International, would lead the investigation into flying wings for decades, until the materials and technology had a chance to catch up.

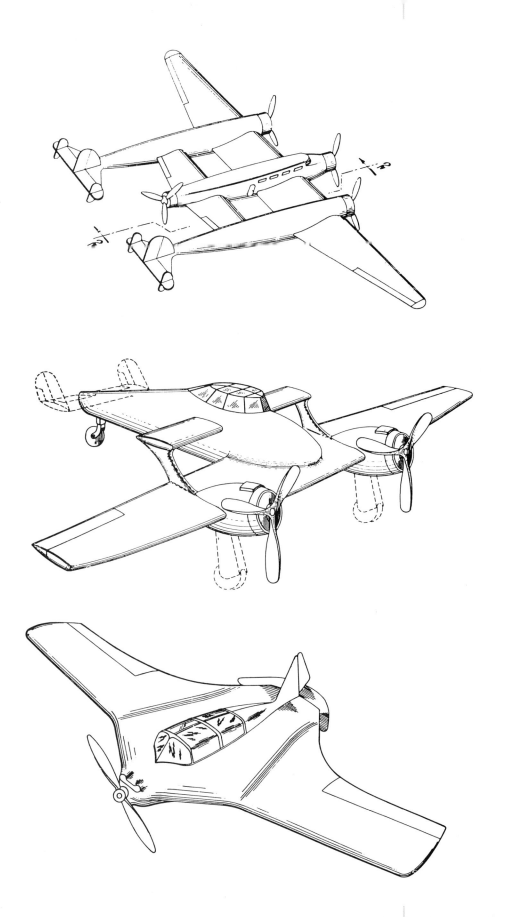

AIRPLANE OR THE LIKE
January 24, 1939
Henry Silverstein
113,019

AIRPLANE OR THE LIKE
December 2, 1941
Henry Silverstein
130,649

AIRPLANE
April 4, 1944
Cheston L. Eshelman
137,628

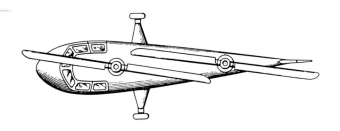
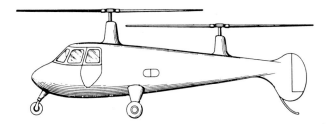

HELICOPTER

February 27, 1945

Othmar F. Maycen

140,480

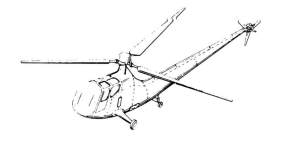

HELICOPTER

June 6, 1944

Igor I. Sikorsky

138,045

HELICOPTER

June 6, 1944

Stanley A. Barshefski

138,034

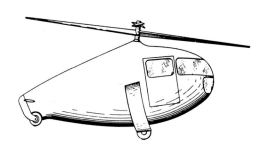
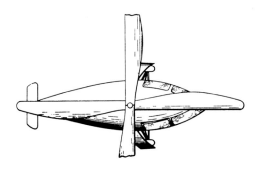

AUTOPLANE

June 21, 1932

Ellsworth W. Carroll

87,201

Fig. 1.

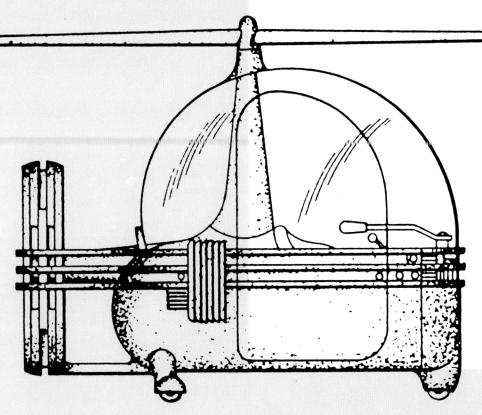

Between Leonardo Da Vinci's drawing of an ascending, spinning screw and Igor I. Sikorsky's patent on the single rotor, all things seemed possible in vertical flight—tailless autoplanes (Des. 87,201), helicopter motorcycles (Des. 140,875), and a host of other hybrids. To some inventors, the helicopter was a dream come true of personal flight—the car of the future.

The helicopter's practical predecessor was Sikorsky's winged and rotored autogyro, developed from the models he made as a boy in Russia. The Russian Revolution sparked his move to the United States and the beginning of a long, successful career in aircraft design. He holds over sixty mechanical and design patents, including those for the quick, maneuverable copters first used in World War II (Des. 138,045).

Fig. 2. *Fig. 3.*

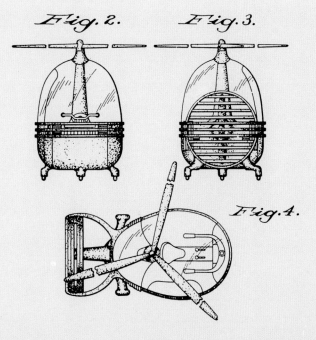

Fig. 4.

HELICOPTER MOTORCYCLE
April 17, 1945
Daniel E. Gumb
140,875

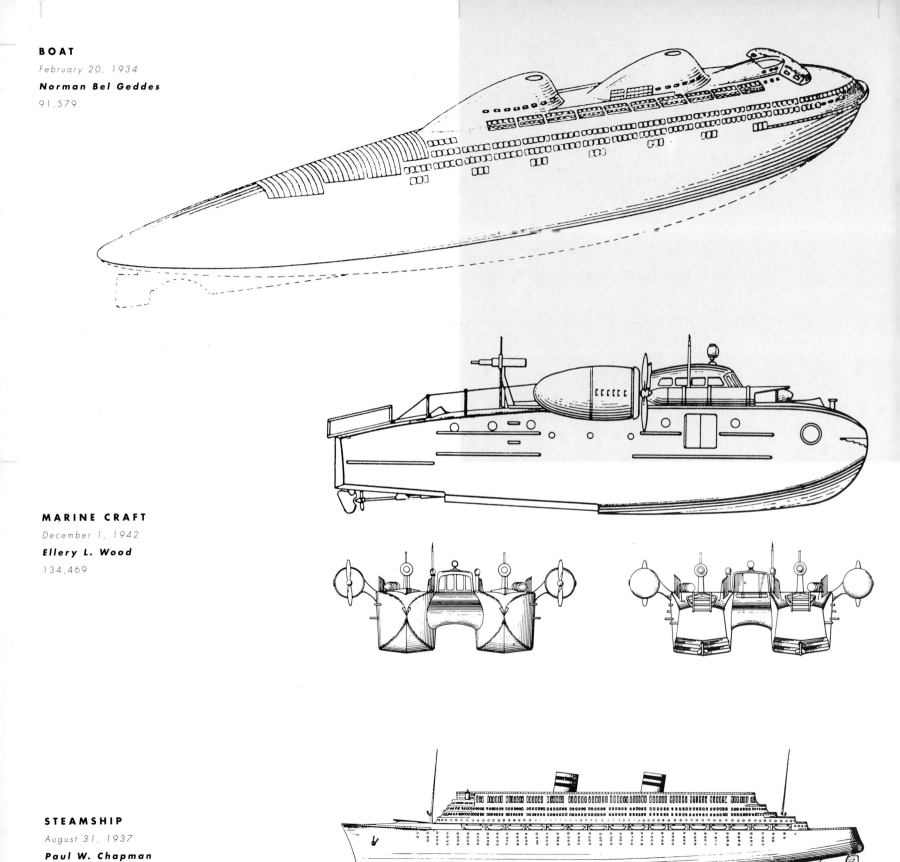

BOAT

February 20, 1934

Norman Bel Geddes

91,579

MARINE CRAFT

December 1, 1942

Ellery L. Wood

134,469

STEAMSHIP

August 31, 1937

Paul W. Chapman

105,841

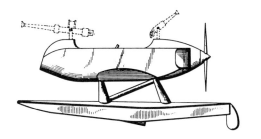

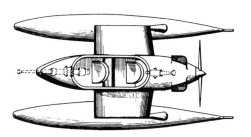

HYDROPLANE

May 30, 1944

Antoine Gazda

137,979

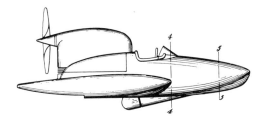

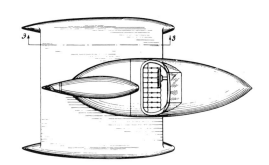

BOAT

October 31, 1939

Walter T. Gassaway

117,415

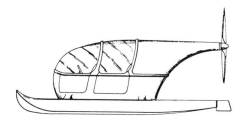

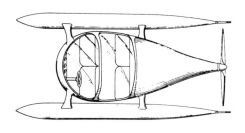

HYDROPLANE OR SIMILAR ARTICLE

June 5, 1945

Raymond C. Baustain

141,506

While working for the Sears, Roebuck
Company, John R. Morgan designed the
Waterwitch outboard motor, a polished
aluminum masterpiece of machine age
craftsmanship which the Museum of
Modern Art saw fit to include in its 1934
Machine Art exhibition. A perfectionist,
Morgan continued to improve on the
motor's design throughout the late 1930s
(Des. 114,597). Other designs for
outboard motors incorporated into their
housing train and automobile grille motifs
(Des. 101,232) or streamlined curves
(Des. 135,329). Even small boat
anchors were given a machine age
treatment: John K. Northrop's 1941
model (Des. 127,184) was as sleek as a
manta ray. The consumer was thus
granted access to the privileges of
advanced design in an affordable realm.

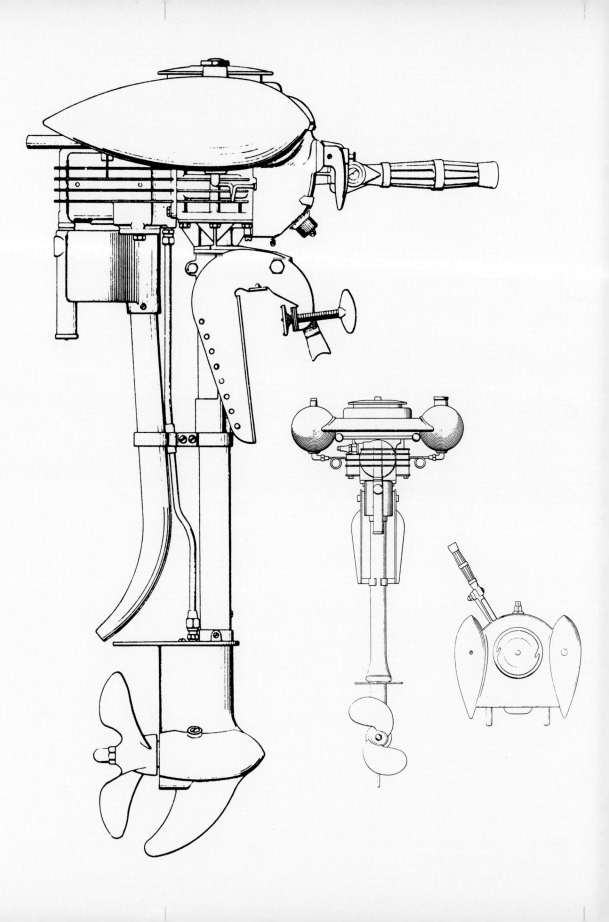

**OUTBOARD MOTOR FOR
BOATS**
May 2, 1939
John R. Morgan
114,597

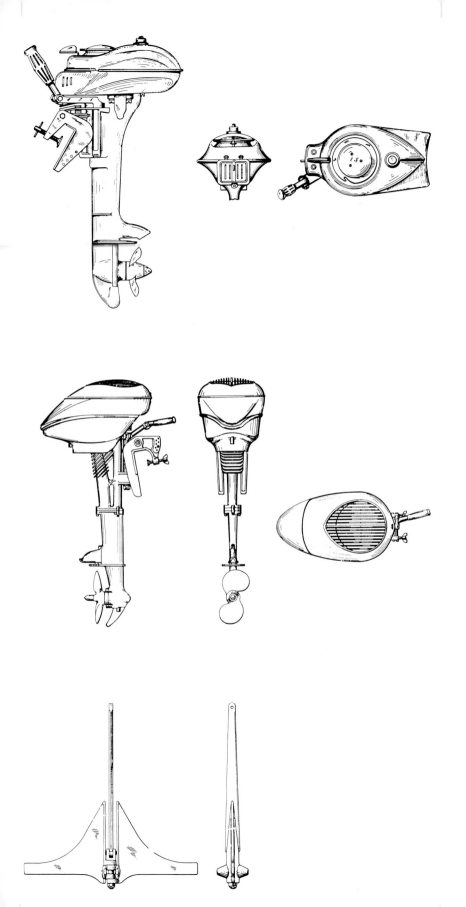

OUTBOARD MOTOR

March 23, 1943

Elmer C. Kiekhaefer

135,329

OUTBOARD MOTOR FOR BOATS

September 15, 1936

Owen C. Linthwaite

101,232

ANCHOR

May 13, 1941

John K. Northrop

127,184

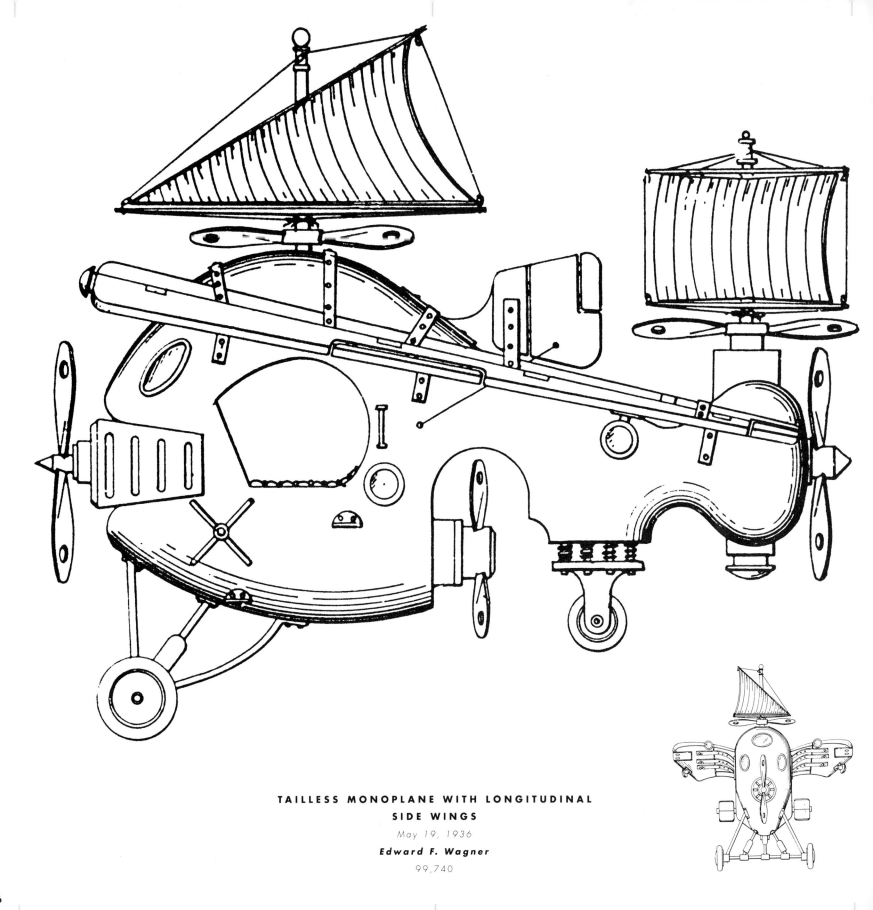

**TAILLESS MONOPLANE WITH LONGITUDINAL
SIDE WINGS**

May 19, 1936

Edward F. Wagner

99,740

**COMBINED AUTOMOBILE,
BOAT, AND AIRPLANE**
January 15, 1935
George Brown
94,329

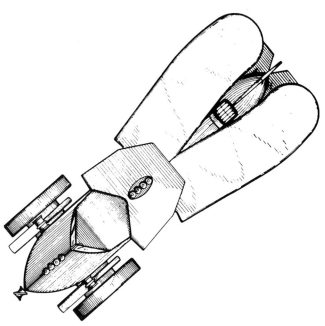

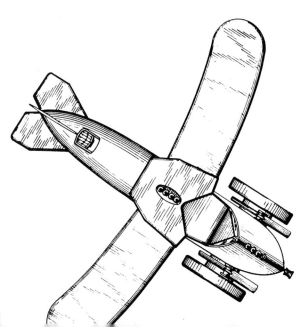

Buckminster Fuller's Dymaxion car was no anomaly. In keeping with the self-taught engineer's credo of building a better society through design, there was a Dymaxion house. Mounted on a central utility pole, suspended on wires, and supported by struts, the round dwelling would combine prefabricated, triangular units from bathroom to den, all factory-made of inexpensive materials. In one of Fuller's plans, a dirigible would scan the globe for a suitable site, a bomb would flatten out the land, poles would be driven in, and the houses hung. A community would be born. ¶ Socio-economic problems in the 1930s aroused in many designers and inventors a drive to construct housing for better living, but Fuller's combination of space-age design, scientific construction methods, and humanistic goals reflected a radical viewpoint. The term dymaxion came from *dynamic*, *maximum*, and *ion*—words combined by a Marshal Field's adman looking for a futuristic label for Fuller's work. Fuller, a visionary in an era infatuated with visions of a new world, had been hired to lecture during the department store's 1929 Modern Furniture exhibition to lend it legitimacy and boost sales. ¶ But Fuller's vision was limited by the fact that few of his patented designs were ever produced; there were others, such as Frank Lloyd Wright, whose designs took more tangible form. His sober reevaluations of proportion—as

seen in his later, streamlined moderne structures—were marked by a horizontal orientation and a measured expansiveness. Horizontality was prevalent in the 1930s, and the fascination with streamlining produced buildings with the trappings of a ship—portholes and deckrailings, stacks and curved corners. Materials used in transportation were translated to fit the modern, suburban home. The "steel house" design patented by Compton is a streamlined unit, covered in a curvy, steel skin. ¶ Shiny, white, and clean: building materials that gave machine age architecture its unadorned elegance also found their way into more commercial designs from the gas station to the diner, where a modern look was tantamount to good, clean service. Opaque, colored glass panels adorned facades of Standard Oil stations and Mom and Pop diners. Stainless steel gave tool cases an efficient-looking sparkle and lunch counters a cheerful shine. ¶ But the diners of the 1930s were not converted cast-offs from the railways, contrary to popular misconceptions. Diner cars took their title from their turn-of-the-century past, when the horse-drawn trolleys made obsolete by streetcar electrification were bought for a pittance and converted into lunch wagons. They were dingy—it was impossible to get out the seasoning from years of public service—and they were disreputable—parked near town squares at all hours of the night, they became hangouts for local toughs, the first customers of the ten-minute meal. ¶ As manufacturing lunch wagons instead of converting them from decrepit streetcars became a growing industry, the process of innovation kicked in. Booths were added to attract women, who felt more secure away from the boisterous counters. Interiors were dolled up. Parked in more respectable areas of town, the diner cars acquired false foundations to hide their wheels, necessary since the only way

STORE FRONT
June 20, 1939
Harry L. Wyman
115,304

to ship a diner was to tow it. The illusion of semi-permanence gave the diner business some stability, and the diners increased in size and inventiveness, imitating long streamliners and depicting settings as fanciful as the South Pole. Though the 1930s still saw diners manufactured with iron wheels, by the end of the decade the diner was on its way to becoming a gleaming and oversized haven, resplendent in Formica and chrome.

DWELLING

April 11, 1939

Frank Lloyd Wright

114,204

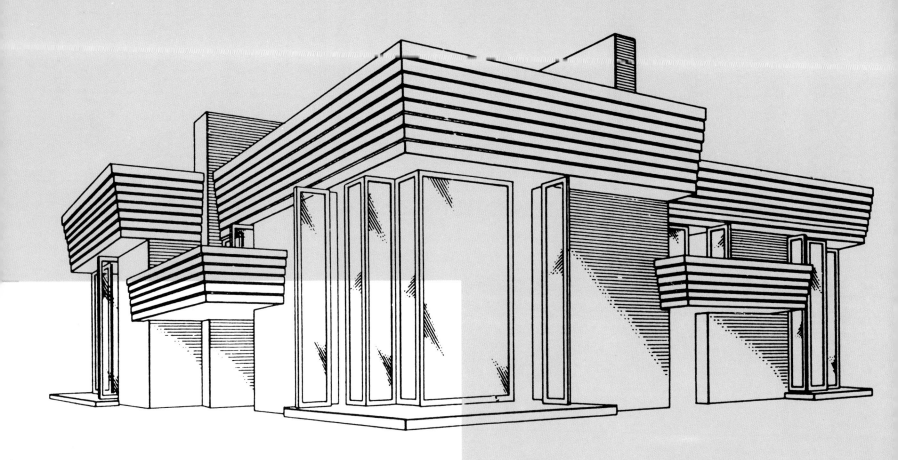

Frank Lloyd Wright's 1939 patent has a balanced precision (Des. 114,204) based on the "clean-cut, straight-line forms" he advocated in an age when machines could produce newly perfect results. Wright saw the drawing-board geometry of his building designs of this period as creating a connection between the tools of design—the T-square and triangle—and the tools of industrial production.

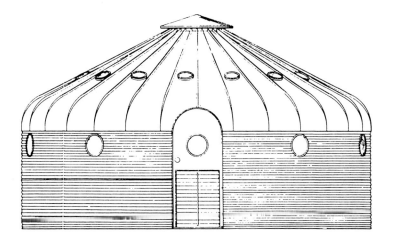

Lacking hard angles but made with a kindred faith in mechanized production, R. Buckminster Fuller's series of "Dymaxion" houses (Des. 133,411) were meant to be factory-made units of modern efficiency for the social good. An aluminum supporting mast contained a triangular elevator and its own utility system which would make the dwelling so warm that blankets and clothes would be unnecessary. The bathroom would be equipped with electric hairclippers and vacuum toothbrushes. Floors would be inflated rubber, walls would be transparent plastic, and the roof would be made of aluminum.

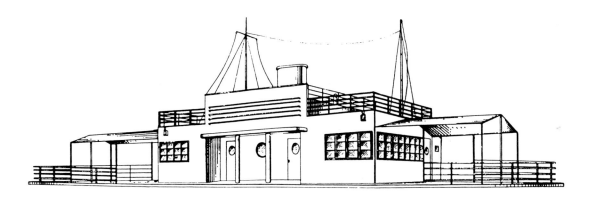

PREFABRICATED HOUSE
August 11, 1942
Richard Buckminster Fuller
133,411

BUILDING
January 21, 1936
George Edwin Brumbaugh
98,210

STEEL HOUSE
October 31, 1939
Beaulard J. Compton
117,422

SERVICE STATION ISLAND OR THE LIKE

April 12, 1938

Alven V. Crouch

109,209

SERVICE STATION

February 18, 1941

Ralph N. Aldrich
Alfred H. Jaehne

125,252

GASOLINE FILLING STATION

March 25, 1941

Batson L. Hewitt

126,073

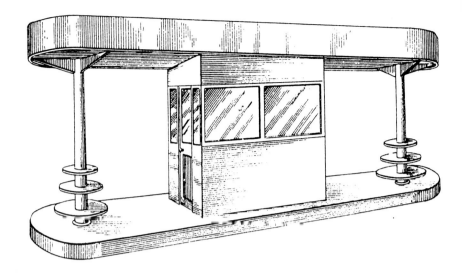

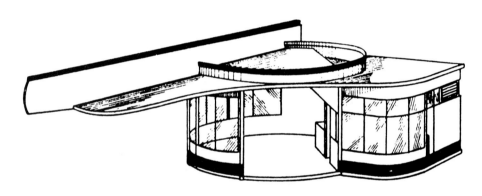

Oil companies first realized the marketing potential of standardized service stations in the 1920s. But the service stations of the next two decades conveyed a sense of uniform reliability and friendliness that transcended the results of their predecessors. Certain materials were crucial to the aura of modern efficiency and hygiene. Porcelain panels in white or bright colors were stacked into sparkling, festive walls (Des. 125,252). Giant glass windows provided sweeping vistas—the better to display the bright, shiny tool cases and products inside. Services themselves were turned into commodities. Texaco, promising clean bathrooms to road-weary travelers, promoted their "Registered Rest Rooms" with advertisements for their "White Patrol," a bathroom inspection team that traversed the country in white cars.

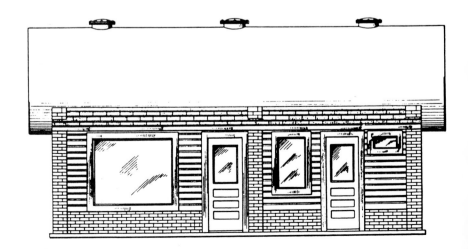

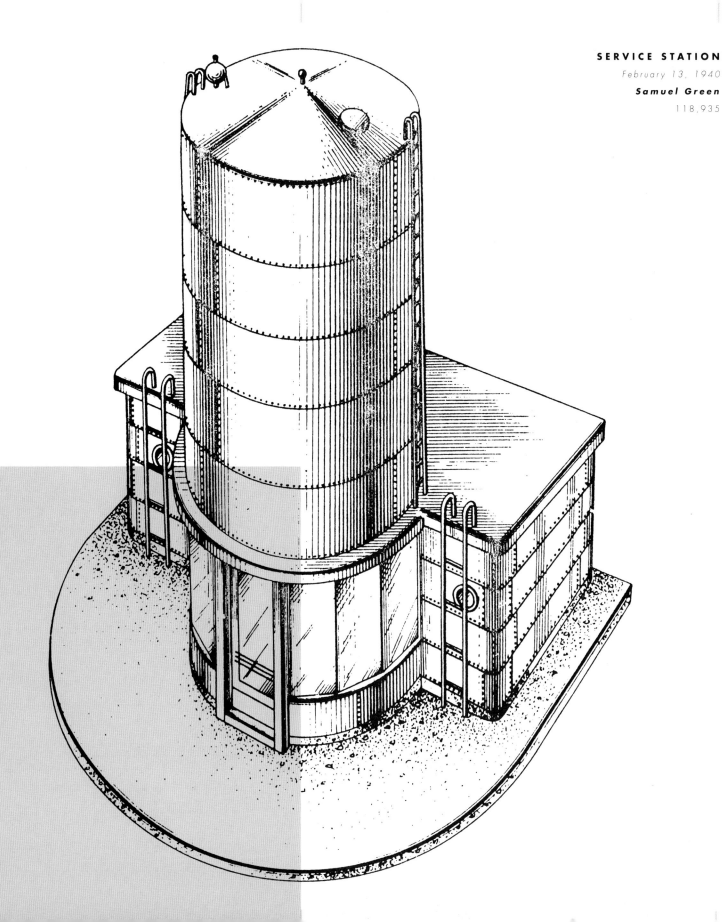

SERVICE STATION RESTAURANT

May 26, 1936

T.T. Record

99,826

BUILDING

December 8, 1936

Robert E. Pellow

102,304

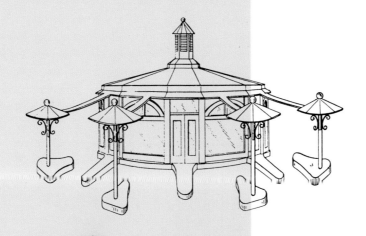

Two icons of America's pioneering spirit sit smack dab against each other in Robert Pellow's 1936 restaurant building (Des. 102,304), which makes reference, conscious or not, to the old horse-drawn lunch wagons that rolled into factory lots in 19th century towns. The long tradition of the lunch wagon (the first was patented in 1891) continued in this 1939 dinette trailer (Des. 115,036). A hungry luncher could pick a stool along the narrow counter and order a bacon sandwich or sardines on rye, a fried egg with a slice of onion on white bread, or coffee and pie.

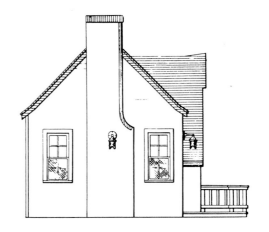

TOURIST CAMP COTTAGE

August 15, 1933

Charles J. Greene

90,484

DINETTE TRAILER

May 30, 1939

Lewis C. Franco

115,036

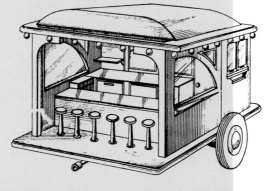

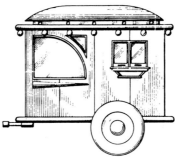

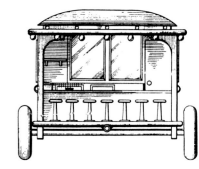

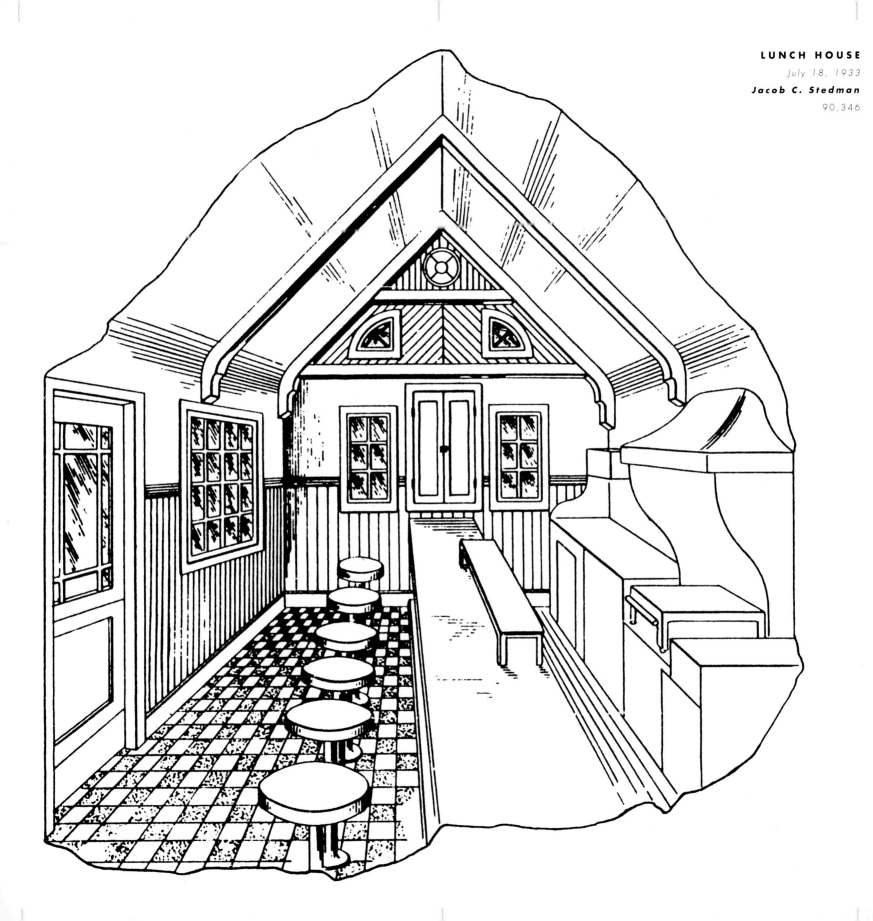

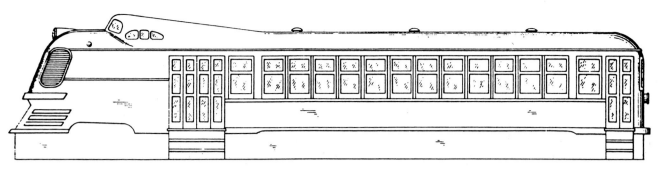

RESTAURANT BUILDING

February 18, 1941

Walter M. Houston

125,271

BUILDING

April 28, 1942

Standish F. Hansell

132,177

DINER

September 12, 1939

Nicholas Caracasis

116,621

RESTAURANT BUILDING
OR SIMILAR ARTICLE
July 18, 1939
Roland L. Stickney
115,803

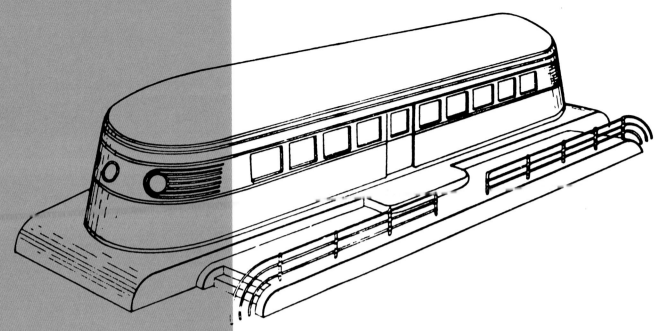

In their homage to the fastest trains of the day and the sheer modernity of streamlining during the machine age, the designers and builders of diners worked with some improbable motifs. The Penguin Diner (Des. 132,177) features a train roaring out of an icy tunnel guarded by a penguin, who stands proud and impervious to the massive clatter happening beneath it. More typical were sleek, space-age shells with sloping sides and roofs as barreled as the roof of a train car.

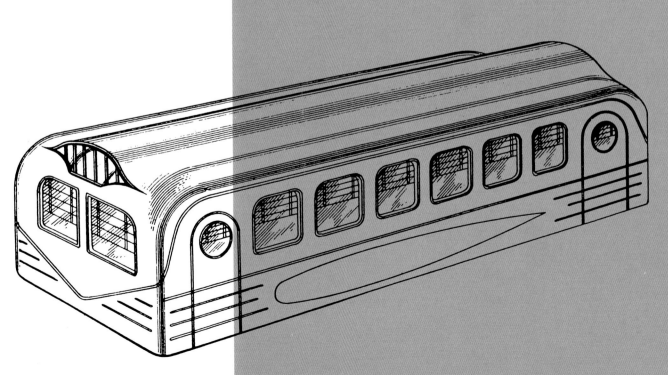

DINER
June 7, 1938
Bertron G. Harley
110,000

BUILDING OF DIRIGIBLE
AIRCRAFT DESIGN

March 29, 1932

Nickolas G. Lagios

86,617

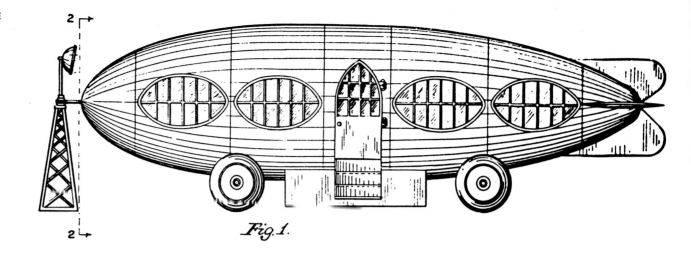

Fig. 1.

Roadside architecture reached a humorous peak in the 1930s. Programmatic buildings featured iconography that was either directly representative, like the Texas barbecue stand (Des. 90,303), or indirectly symbolic, like the dirigible diner (Des. 86,617), which serves up its own version of what the modern, streamlined diner form should be. Instead of assuming the shape of an earth-bound train it went straight into the air. A vernacular took shape along America's roads that said "coffee here," "we serve corn," and "have a donut" with unmistakable clarity.

BUILDING

April 5, 1932

Sadie O'Neil

86,683

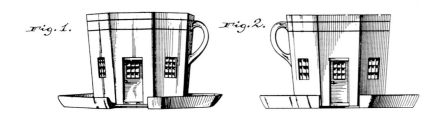

BUILDING
December 21, 1937
Daniel G. Terrie
107,561

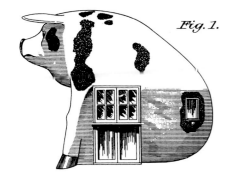

BARBECUE STAND
July 18, 1933
W.H. Alston
90,303

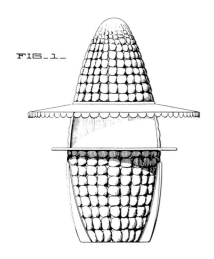

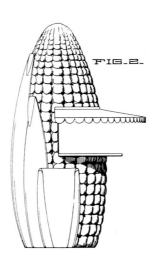

BOOTH
July 7, 1936
J.M. Miller
100,333

BUILDING
January 12, 1932
Jerome Watt
86,001

It was 1939. America was on its way to recovery, the worst of the Depression over. It was a year which celebrated progress with two world's fairs. On Long Island, Mr. Levitt completed the model home for his new development and planned a fantastic opening day. He wrapped the new house in cellophane—that wonder material from the Chicago exposition of 1933. Then he topped the wrapping with a giant bow, invited in the throngs, and had the entire chorus line of Broadway's *Babes in Arms* unveil the new home with a set of colossal scissors. Levittown was inaugurated in a flourish of publicity. ¶ Equipping the home in the 1930s was an entirely new endeavor. Unfamiliar gadgets were promoted as modern improvements for the housewife's lot. Familiar items such as toasters—suddenly clothed in shiny, smooth housings with Bakelite knobs and chromium dials—were hailed as vital work-savers. Whether or not the redesign of a familiar item made it more effective or easier to use was not the question to ask. The real question was, how could one run a modern home without the latest conveniences? ¶ Laden with products whose quaint forms seemed only to remind consumers of hard times, manufacturers were quick to change their thinking. That the shift from traditional comforts to modern conveniences took place first in the kitchen and the bathroom had much to do with a new national awareness of the importance of hygiene. The pared-down surface of a shiny new stove was decidedly easier to clean. ¶ "I am a General Electric dishwasher," a voice intoned as a washing machine started itself and an electric stove door opened and closed. This was no housewife's nightmare, but an exhibit in Chicago's 1933 Century of Progress Exposition, which featured electricity itself as the star of the show. After reshaping a slew of products and deinstitutionalizing the clunky forms of heavy appliances, industrial designers often stayed around to design the booth at the fair. For some, like Henry Dreyfuss, this was a natural course: he started in stage sets and never forgot the value of a great presentation. Words like "hygiene" and "convenience" took center stage along with the products that embodied them. "Improved" was another key term. Across the country individual inventors took the cue and toiled away in their basement workshops, facing magazine clippings that proclaimed nothing would reap fame and profit like a home appliance. In this era of progress, it was practically every inventor's duty to think hard about a better mousetrap. ¶ The Levittown housewife had probably grown accustomed to her new liberation by 1939—made possible by a modular kitchen or the "cleanlined" surfaces of a bathroom full of Dreyfuss-designed Crane fixtures. Most likely both rooms were bright as lightbulbs:

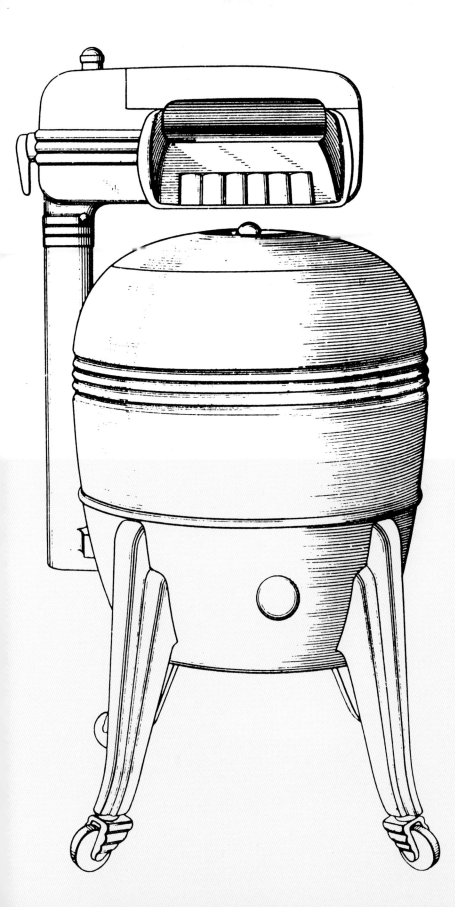

**COMBINED WASHING
MACHINE CASING AND
WRINGER**

June 2, 1936

John R. Morgan

99,888

the electrification of the American home rose from 24% in 1917 to 90% in 1940. The resulting light flooded living areas as well, chasing away the shadows and making fusty comforts unnecessary requirements for feeling at home. The shift from Victorian bulk to machine-age elegance took place in a pool of incandescent light. ¶ Russel Wright designed his American modern furniture in shades of light wood, upholstered in bright plaids—ideal for a new surburban home. One could serve cocktails in a room of tubular chrome and leather chairs—once thought too hard-looking for home use—or flick the ash of a *Lucky Strike* into the bowl of a smoking stand by Wolfgang Hoffman. These were among the best examples of the craftsmanship of the machine age—a harmony of new materials and modern visions, mass-produced with mechanical precision.

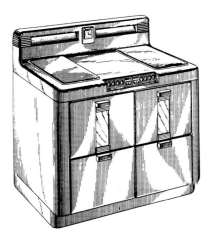

COOKING STOVE
December 16, 1941
William H. Stangle
130,802

John Tjaarda's appliances for Briggs Manufacturing expressed the new machine aesthetic in domestic form. The Briggs's "Kitchen of Tomorrow," introduced in 1935, had a cylindrical electric range (Des. 98,411) that sat in the middle of a sleek linoleum floor against the understated backdrop of modular kitchen cabinets. The stove was lit by a lamp that rose up from its center like a periscope. Tjaarda's 1939 design for a modular kitchen unit (Des. 115,826) reflected a more practical concept of modern convenience and efficiency.

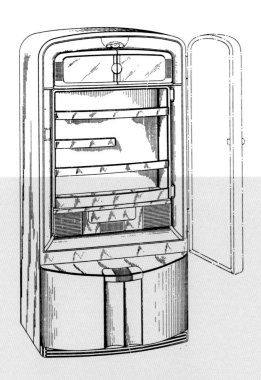

DOMESTIC REFRIGERATOR
January 13, 1942
Harold L. Van Doren
131,103

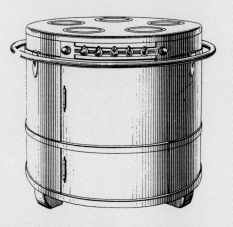

STOVE
January 28, 1936
John Tjaarda
98,411

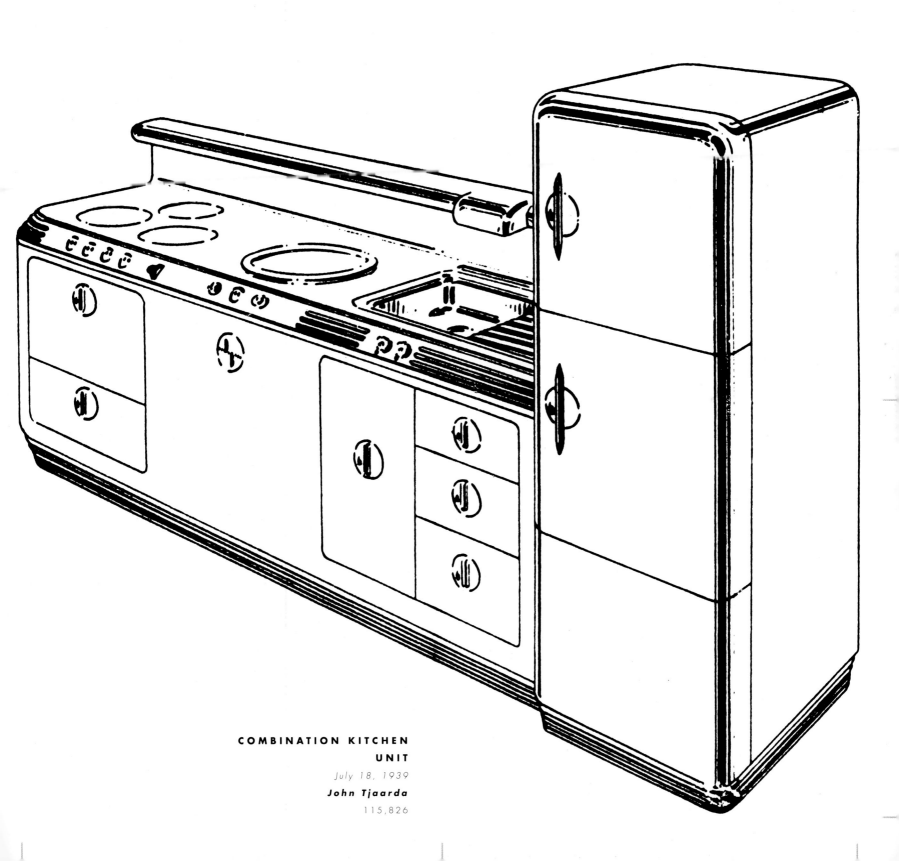

**COMBINATION KITCHEN
UNIT**
July 18, 1939
John Tjaarda
115,826

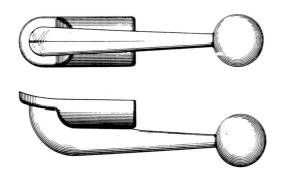

DOOR HANDLE
October 31, 1939
Raymond Loewy
117,380

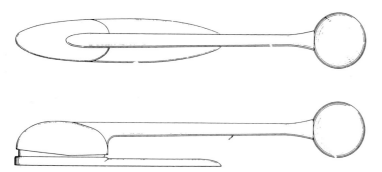

**COMBINED DOOR LATCH
HANDLE AND MOUNTING
FOR REFRIGERATOR OR
THE LIKE**
January 7, 1941
John R. Morgan
124,538

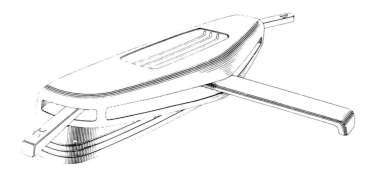

PLUMBING FIXTURE
July 3, 1934
John Tjaarda
92,687

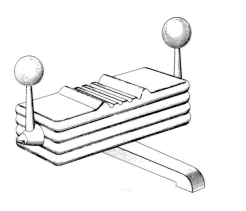

FAUCET
June 12, 1934
Raymond Loewy
92,480

KITCHEN CABINET ENSEMBLE

March 9, 1937

John R. Morgan

103,501

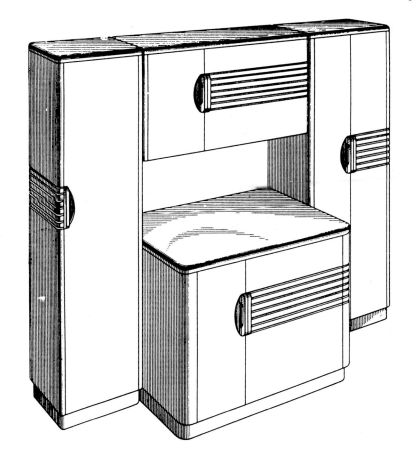

After Henry Dreyfuss turned the Sears Coldspot contract down he recommended Raymond Loewy, who was hired for $2,500. Loewy helped Sears establish itself as a major appliance manufacturer. Unit sales of the redesigned refrigerator jumped from 15,000 to 275,000 in five years. Even the door handle (Des. 117,380) looked racy. Its sphere and stem design, appropriate in the trylon and perisphere-dominated year of the world's fair, was later adapted and restrained by John Morgan (Des. 124,538), who ran Sears' first industrial design department.

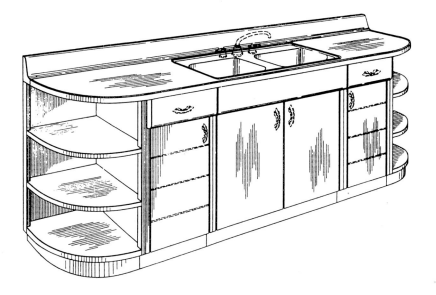

COMBINED SINK AND CABINET

March 13, 1945

Jacques Stanitz

140,574

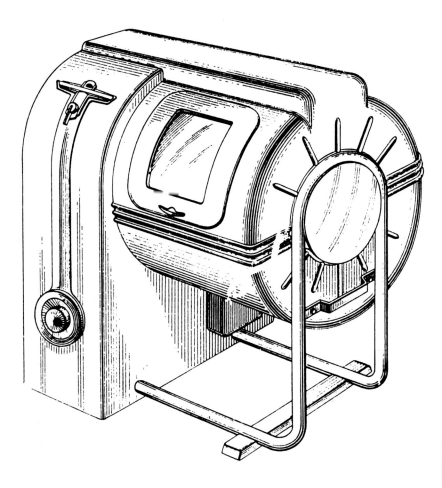

WASHING MACHINE CABINET
November 14, 1939
Hyman D. Brotman
117,627

WASHING MACHINE CABINET
July 6, 1937
Amos E. Northrup
105,228

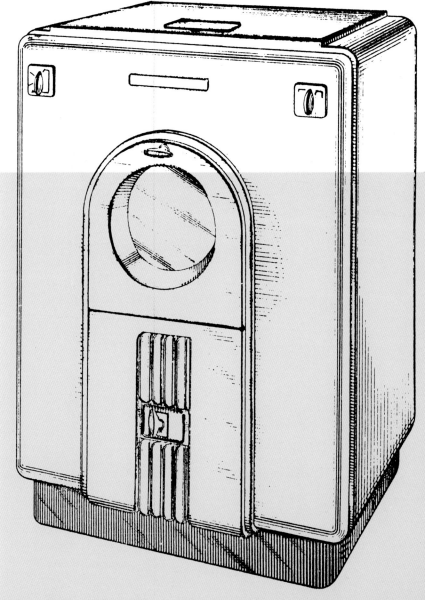

Henry Dreyfuss's "cleanlined" bathroom fixtures for the Crane Company, 1936 (Des. 101,446; 101,447; and 101,441), were conceived with characteristic consideration for the human beings that would use them. As he wrote in *Designing for People,* "No one knows for sure why bathtubs were set on iron claw legs, forming a difficult dirt pocket underneath. Nor why ceramic basins were cemented under a hole in a marble slab, forming a hidden grease pocket around the joint. Today most people do their own housework and when we take a bathroom-design assignment we want to know how easy it can be kept clean . . ."

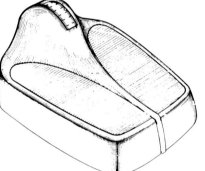

**COMBINED LAVATORY
AND PEDESTAL**
October 6, 1936
Henry Dreyfuss
Roy H. Zinkil
101,446

BATHTUB
October 6, 1936
Henry Dreyfuss
Roy H. Zinkil
101,447

WATER CLOSET
October 6, 1936
Henry Dreyfuss
101,441

SCALE
May 17, 1938
Max Garbell
109,710

**WEIGHING SCALE OR
SIMILAR ARTICLE**
December 8, 1936
William H. Greenleaf
102,272

WEIGHING SCALE
May 19, 1936
Russell E. Vanderhoff
Mathias J. Weber
99,738

BATHROOM SCALE
May 30, 1944
Carl. W. Sundberg
137,990

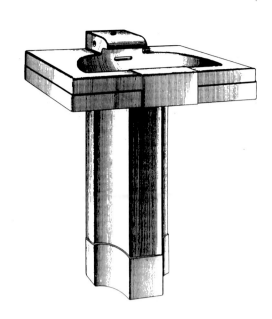

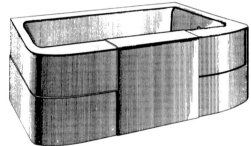

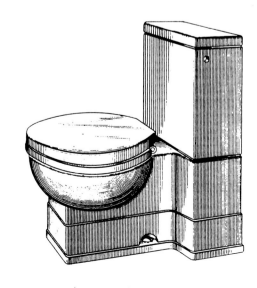

ELECTRIC FOOD MIXER

March 31, 1942

Hermann M. Alfred Strauss

131,792

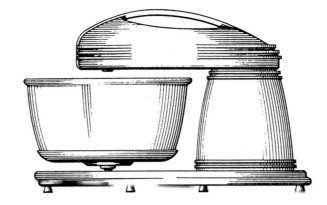

DRINK MIXER

December 26, 1939

James F. Barnes

Jean Otis Reinecke

118,225

Chicago designers James Barnes and
Jean Reinecke updated the classic
Hamilton Beach Drinkmaster in 1939,
adding curve and taper to the chrome
motor housing where it met the mixing
stem (Des. 118,225).

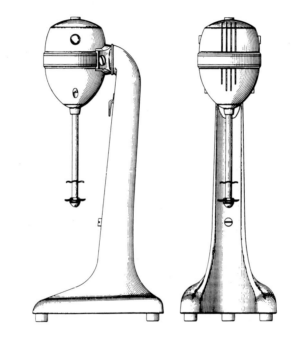

ELECTRIC FOOD MIXER

July 7, 1942

Chauncey E. Waltman

132,968

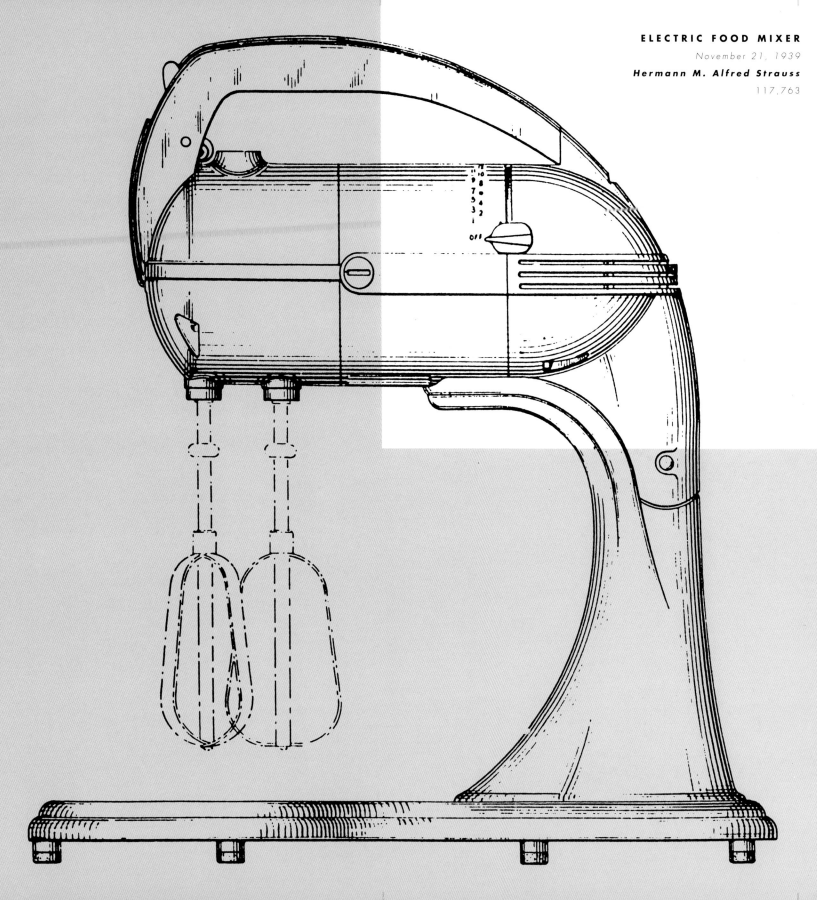

ELECTRIC FOOD MIXER
November 21, 1939
Hermann M. Alfred Strauss
117,763

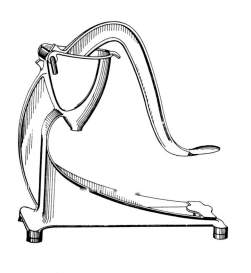

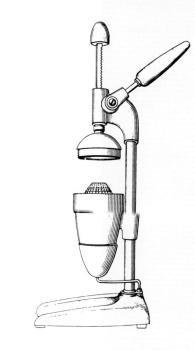

JUICE EXTRACTOR

February 16, 1932

George W. Bungay

86,217

FRUIT JUICE EXTRACTOR

July 4, 1939

James F. Barnes

Jean Otis Reinecke

115,487

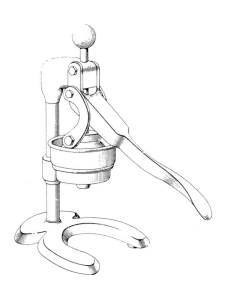

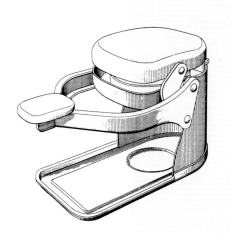

**FRUIT JUICE EXTRACTOR
OR THE LIKE**

July 1, 1941

Raymond Zurawin

127,985

JUICE EXTRACTOR

December 2, 1941

Walter H. Pleiss

130,573

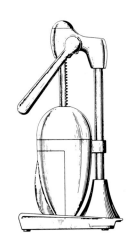

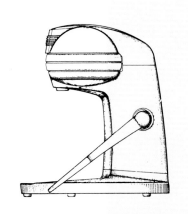

FRUIT JUICE EXTRACTOR

June 9, 1942

Henry J. Talge

132,678

JUICE EXTRACTOR

February 6, 1945

Dave Chapman

140,239

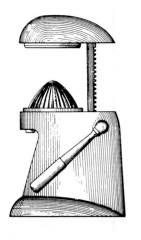

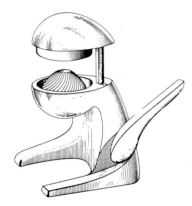

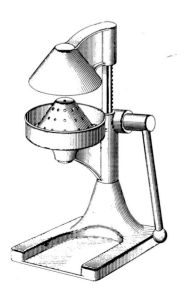

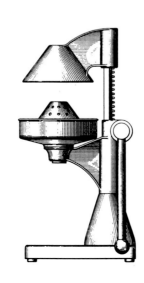

"A person finds something he's using doesn't work right, or it's clumsy, or costs too much. He gets a happy thought. He improves the old Article. That's [a] contribution to human progress. That's the way that many, many men have reached the goal of financial comfort, independence and even wealth. Most of the things millions of us use didn't come from the brains of engineers and physicists. They came from the mind and maybe the crude home work bench of Mr. Average Man, busily engaged in earning his bread and butter at whatever chance or circumstance has given him to do. The 'little' man's opportunity as an inventor was never greater than it is today."—*1935 Advertisement in Modern Mechanix by Victor J. Evans & Co., Registered Patent Attorneys, Washington, D.C.*

FRUIT JUICE EXTRACTOR
May 15, 1945
William E. Maxson, Jr.
141,241

JUICE EXTRACTOR
February 6, 1945
Ray Abraham
140,237

JUICE EXTRACTOR
August 25, 1936
Herbert C. Johnson
101,000

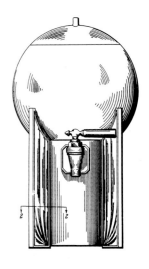

The ritual of making coffee found its expression in a number of forms, from Ambrose Olds's machine of 1932 (Des. 86,967), whose globe urn and unadorned spigot makes clear its mechanical, electrical function, to George Scharfenberg's 1937 percolator (Des. 104,477), whose twin coffeepots express the freer geometry of a country in slightly better shape. Peter Schlumbohm's organic and elegant Chemex of 1940 (Des. 137,943), needing no power and made of Pyrex and wood, expresses a philosophy of scientific simplicity. Schlumbohm, who by his death in 1962 held more than 300 patents, referred to all his work as inventions, despising the term designer for its parasitic connotations.

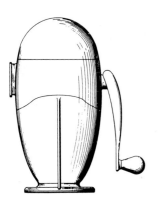

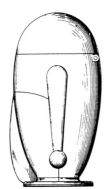

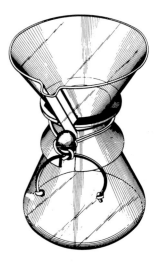

COFFEE MAKER
May 17, 1932
Ambrose D. Olds
86,967

COFFEE MAKER OR THE LIKE
May 11, 1937
George T. Scharfenberg
104,477

SYPHON
September 29, 1936
L.T. Ward
101,421

ICE CRUSHER
February 27, 1945
Henry J. Talge
140,454

COCKTAIL SHAKER OR SIMILAR ARTICLE
October 13, 1936
Emil A. Schuelke
101,559

COMBINED FLASK AND HANDLE, FOR A COFFEEMAKER OR THE LIKE
May 23, 1944
Peter Schlumbohm
137,943

Patentable subject matter has long been an issue with the U.S. Patent Office, but it was not until 1952 that an effective clause on offensiveness was adopted. What was accepted once is not accepted now.

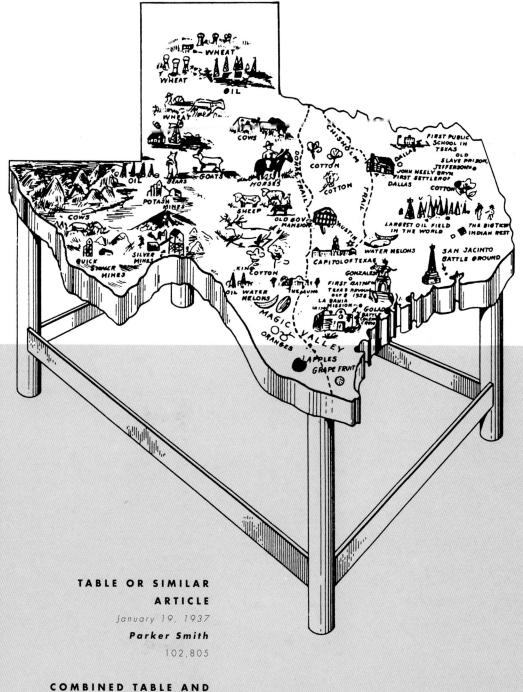

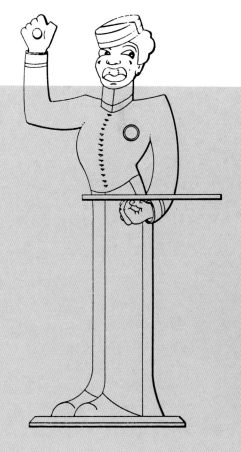

TABLE OR SIMILAR ARTICLE
January 19, 1937
Parker Smith
102,805

COMBINED TABLE AND RACK
April 19, 1932
Rudolph Berliner
86,760

CLOCK CASE

June 7, 1932

Alva H. Schick
Randolph P. Kraatz

87,132

CLOCK CASING

April 11, 1939

Henry Dreyfuss

114,262

SHIP CLOCK

April 15, 1941

Abraham Levy
Joseph F. Punzak

126,627

CLOCKCASE

May 20, 1941

Leo Ivan Bruce

127,367

CLOCK OR SIMILAR ARTICLE

April 15, 1941

Kate Lerman

126,611

CLOCK

January 24, 1939

Joseph L. Stone

113,022

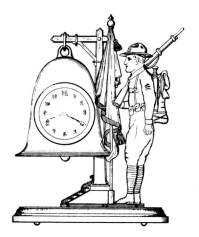

ELECTRIC CLOCK

March 25, 1941

Norman Lipsky

126,049

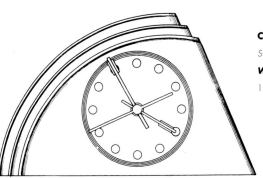

CLOCK

September 14, 1937

William E. Hentschel

106,041

GLOBE CLOCK

January 12, 1937

Abe Leonard Koolish

102,690

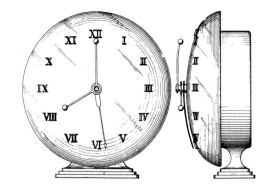

CLOCK

January 7, 1936

Arnold S. Rittenberg

98,089

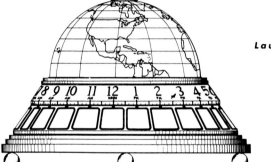

WORLD CLOCK

April 16, 1935

Laurence S. Harrison

95,205

**COMBINATION CLOCK
AND CALENDAR**

July 12, 1938

Herbert W. Lamport

110,489

CLOCK

June 17, 1941

**Alexander R. Tigerman
Milton N. Tigerman**

127,848

**COMBINED LAMP, RADIO,
AND CLOCK**

January 9, 1940

**T. Tinker
G. von der Lin**

118,550

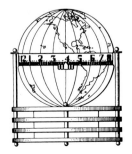

CLOCK

January 12, 1937

Ossian K. Mitchell

102,697

**COMBINATION CLOCK
AND CALENDAR**

December 29, 1936

Joseph C. Morris

102,573

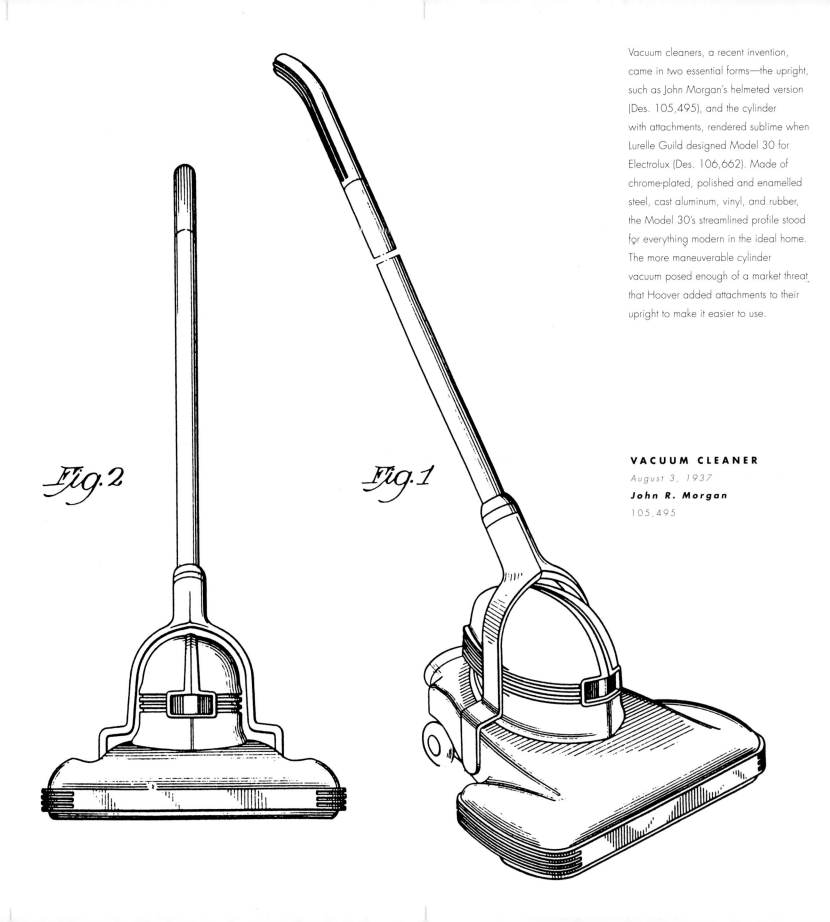

Vacuum cleaners, a recent invention, came in two essential forms—the upright, such as John Morgan's helmeted version (Des. 105,495), and the cylinder with attachments, rendered sublime when Lurelle Guild designed Model 30 for Electrolux (Des. 106,662). Made of chrome-plated, polished and enamelled steel, cast aluminum, vinyl, and rubber, the Model 30's streamlined profile stood for everything modern in the ideal home. The more maneuverable cylinder vacuum posed enough of a market threat that Hoover added attachments to their upright to make it easier to use.

Fig. 2

Fig. 1

VACUUM CLEANER
August 3, 1937
John R. Morgan
105,495

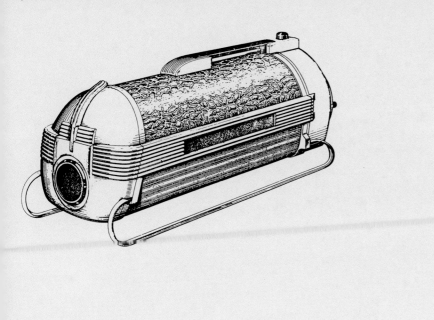

**VACUUM CLEANER
CASING**
October 26, 1937
Lurelle Guild
106,662

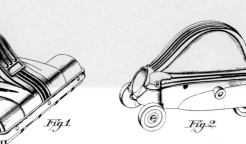

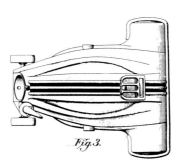

**VACUUM CLEANER
CASING**
May 19, 1936
Malcom S. Park
99,723

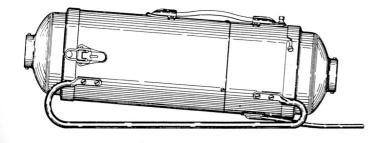

SUCTION CLEANER
November 21, 1939
Eugene F. Martinet
117,775

CHAIR
February 25, 1941
Thomas L. Hand
125,471

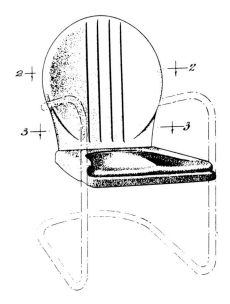

CHAIR
July 5, 1938
James F. Eppenstein
110,387

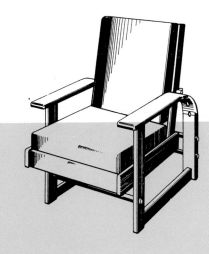

ADJUSTABLE CHAIR
February 18, 1936
Russel Wright
98,637

FOLDING CHAIR
December 19, 1939
Willard H. Bond, Jr.
118,185

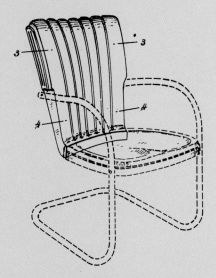

CHAIR
January 16, 1940
Walter D. Teague
118,610

ARMCHAIR
May 5, 1936
Milton B. Smith
99,556

CHAIR

November 24, 1936

Wolfgang Hoffman

102,030

LOUNGE CHAIR

February 11, 1936

Wolfgang Hoffman

98,518

LAWN CHAIR

January 12, 1932

A.O. Wilkening

86,003

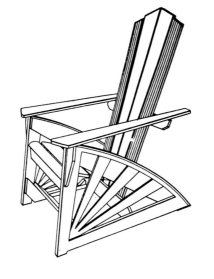

CHAIR

September 22, 1942

Alexey Brodovitch

133,847

GLIDER

June 8, 1943

William I. Smith

135,777

LOUNGE CHAIR

February 11, 1936

Wolfgang Hoffman

98,517

CHAISE LOUNGE FRAME
May 26, 1936

Wolfgang Hoffman

99,803

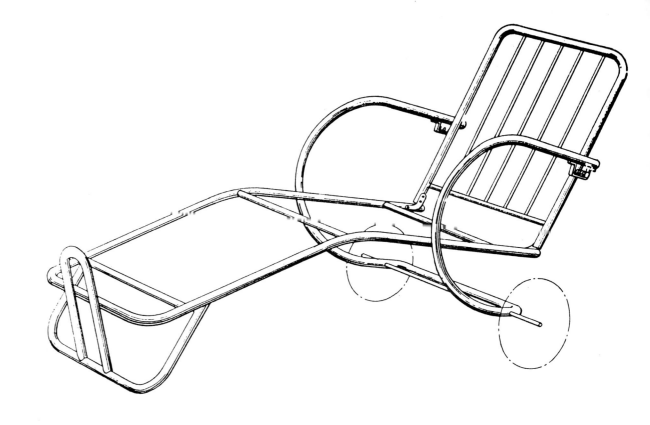

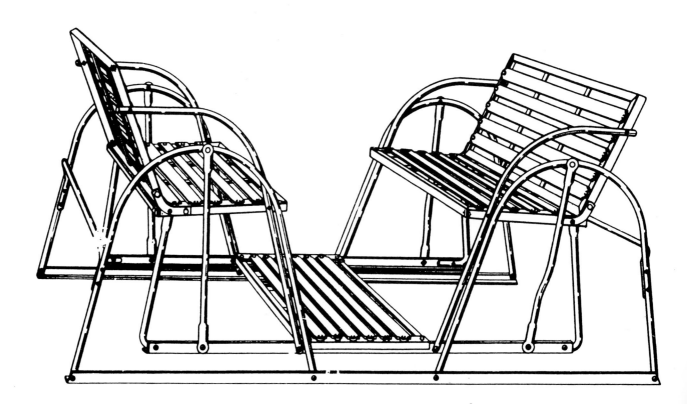

SWING
November 14, 1939

William I. Smith

117,622

CHAIR
March 16, 1937
Richard B. Janes
103,575

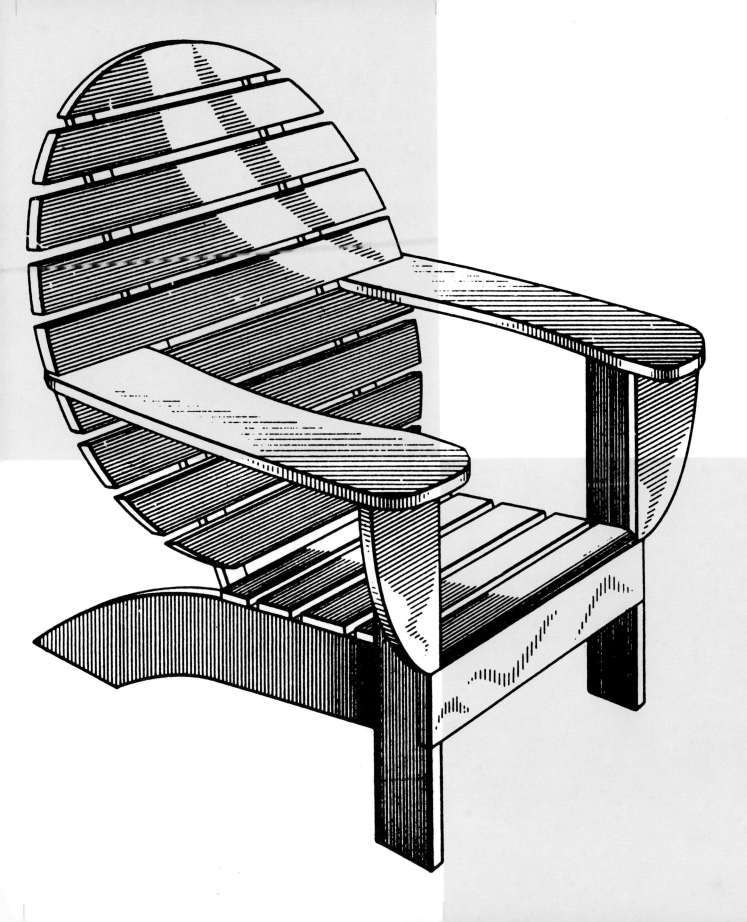

Joe was 5'10". Josephine was 5'5". Just an average couple holding down a variety of jobs, from factory-work to office-work—sitting, standing, reading, and typing. In their own, average way, they were trend-setters. With them lay the answers to the most pressing questions. Exactly how high and wide was the ideal dentist's chair, or a shoe salesman's bench, or a telephone operator's stool? And what were the best angles for these fundamental components of modern commerce? Just how long is the average female's jawline, from chin to ear? How long is a man's forearm? ¶ It was human and not just aesthetic interest that prompted Henry Dreyfuss and his firm to conjure up Joe and Josephine, send them to work, put them on planes, and even give them children. As ergometric models, Dreyfuss's family were members of a new, friendlier world, where work would fit people and not the other way around, where work would be comfortable—and in Dreyfuss's mind, not only more efficient, but more productive. Other industrial designers may have been compelled by a different set of standards in the drive towards modernization. But Dreyfuss's unflagging faith that greater comfort would result in productivity won him contracts. There was no harm in the elegance and style of his designs either, or in his conception of "survival form"—in which a new design contains enough vestiges of the old to seem a familiar and usable item. Even his checkwriter embodies a feeling of modern, businesslike ease. ¶ The machine age brought functional innovations to industry, to be sure—from the newly improved Bell telephone to Parker's fast-drying fountain pen inks. But in the housings, though not necessarily the workings, of virtually all an office's accessories lay the truest expression of modernity. Save for a few changes, the stapler of 1940 did the same things as the stapler of 1920. But give its shell a racy taper, its base the outline of a teardrop, its hinge cover the shape of a car's wheel cowl—complete with speed stripes—make its handle so rounded yet flat it suggests a breakthrough in vertical flight, and you'll find the real geometry of efficency. Redesigned, even the smallest tool in a clerk's arsenal turned his desk into a landing strip. ¶ Would a stapler that practically rushed forward with the deft grace of modern momentum generate more momentum in its user? Certainly no one expected such a direct effect. But it might generate some pride—might prompt the night maid to spend a minute polishing the shine back into the office's new streamlined hole puncher. A public that had wandered the expanse of the New York

World's Fair would remember the magnificent cash register building that housed the latest in Walter Dorwin Teague's designs for National Cash Register, if for the novelty alone. But the business community would remember it for something else. And what

STAPLING MACHINE
February 20, 1940
Charles I. Tager
119,078

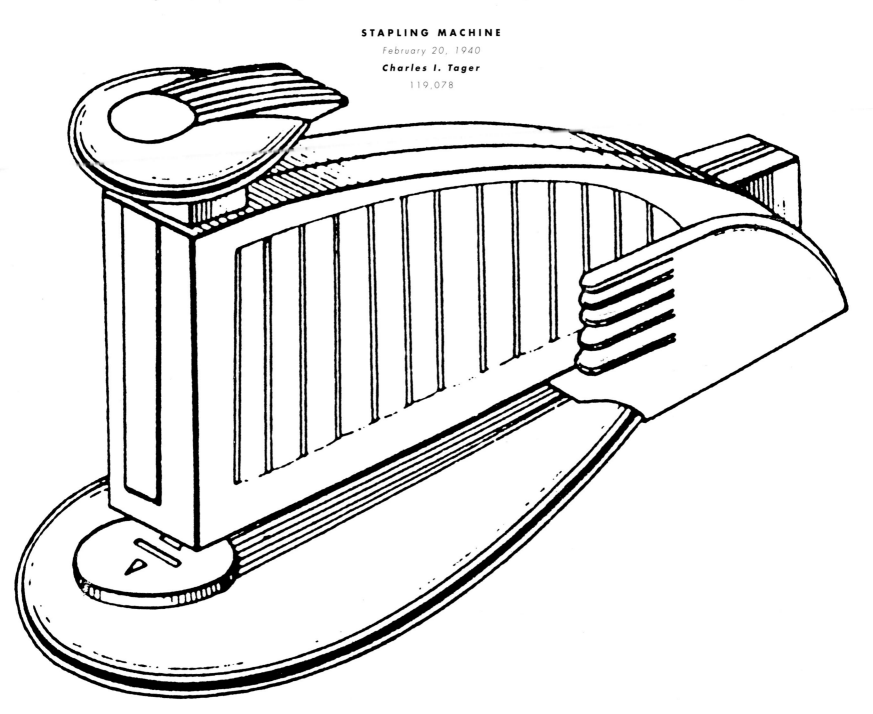

a glorification of commerce the company showroom in Rockefeller Center was, with its stainless steel and glass facade, the models proudly displayed inside theatrically lit potholes. In such a charismatic setting, business began to take on a 20th century glamour.

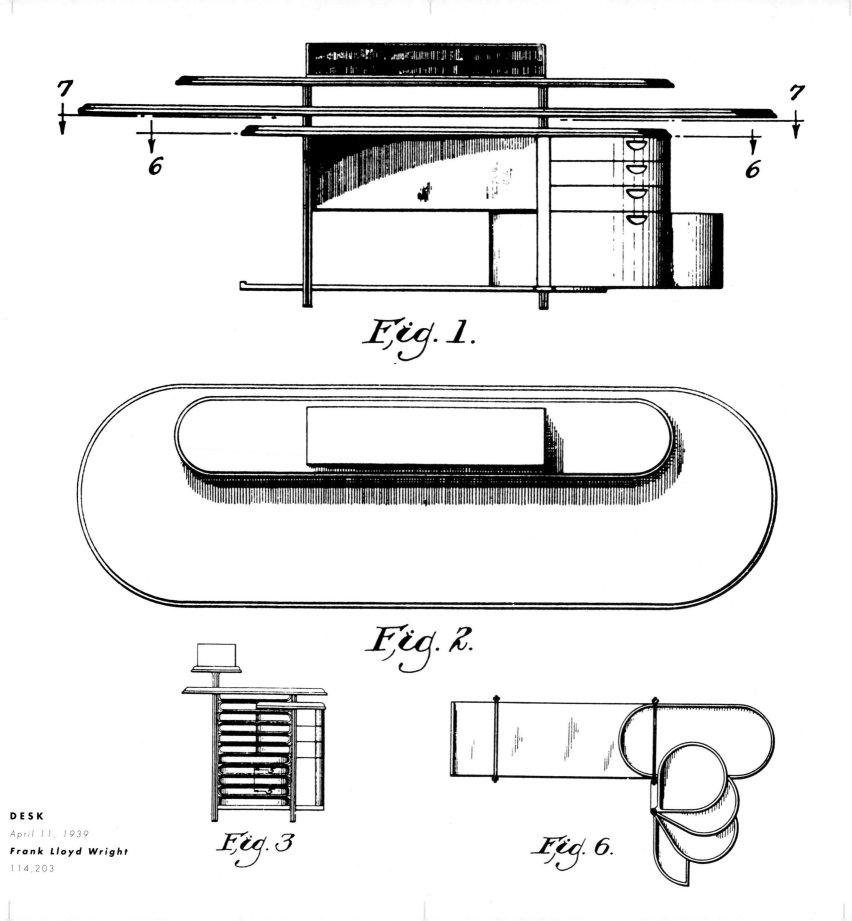

Fig. 1.

Fig. 2.

Fig. 3

Fig. 6.

DESK
April 11, 1939
Frank Lloyd Wright
114,203

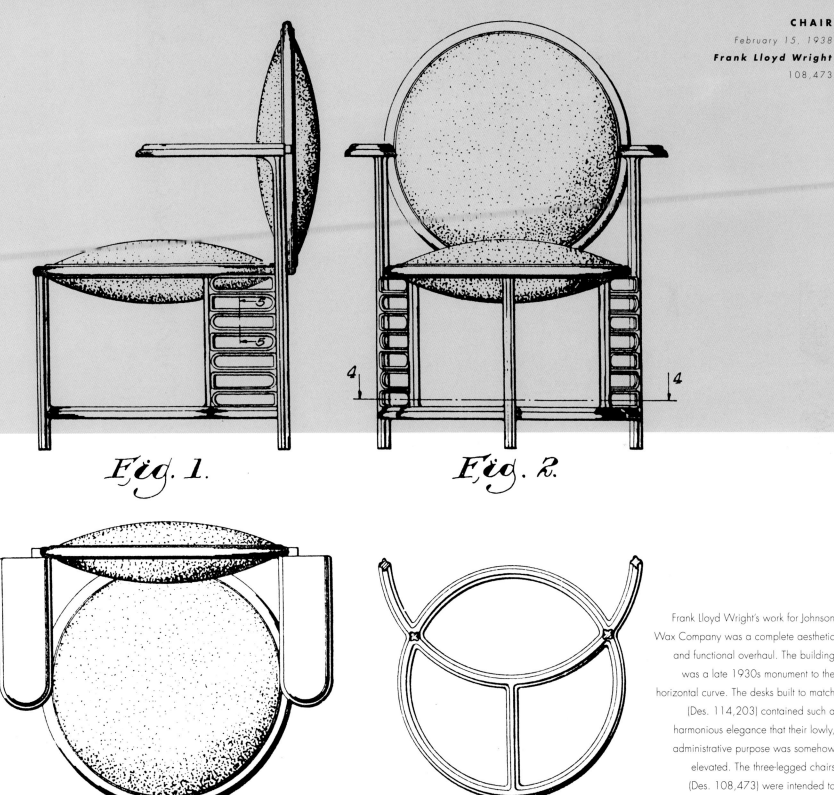

CHAIR
February 15, 1938
Frank Lloyd Wright
108,473

Fig. 1.

Fig. 2.

Fig. 3.

Fig. 4.

Frank Lloyd Wright's work for Johnson Wax Company was a complete aesthetic and functional overhaul. The building was a late 1930s monument to the horizontal curve. The desks built to match (Des. 114,203) contained such a harmonious elegance that their lowly, administrative purpose was somehow elevated. The three-legged chairs (Des. 108,473) were intended to promote efficiency and good posture: if the typist did not sit up straight, the chair would tip over.

PENCIL SHARPENER
March 6, 1934
Raymond Loewy
91,675

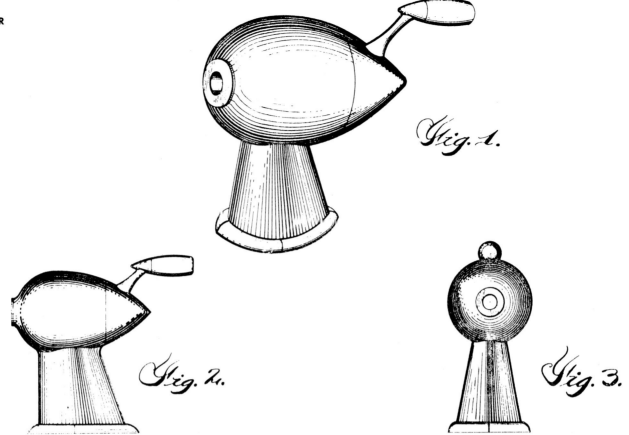

Fig. 1.

Fig. 2.

Fig. 3.

" . . . fountain pens and pencil sharpeners were stupidly modeled after the teardrop, which was held up as an ideal form, one which a body free to change its shape would assume in order to offer a minimum of resistance to air. Some critics pointed out that fountain pens and baby buggies seldom stirred up much of a breeze, and a streamlined pencil sharpener couldn't get away if it tried . . . Needless streamlining was made even more ridiculous when high-speed photography revealed that the teardrop form was an optical illusion . . ."
—Henry Dreyfuss, Designing for People

FOUNTAIN PEN
June 16, 1931
Andreas Beinenstein
84,394

PENCIL
April 21, 1936
Frank C. Deli
99,346

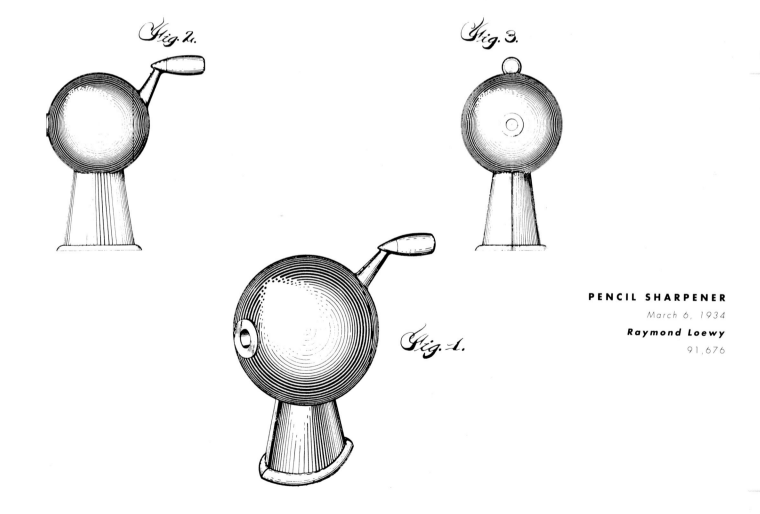

Fig. 2.

Fig. 3.

Fig. 1.

PENCIL SHARPENER
March 6, 1934
Raymond Loewy
91,676

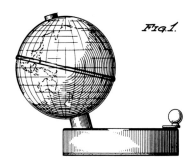

FIG.1.

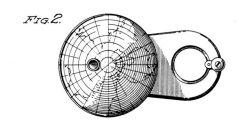

FIG.2.

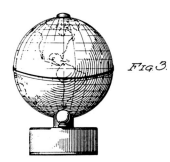

FIG.3.

**PENCIL SHARPENING
DEVICE**
March 10, 1936
Herman Lobel
Louis DiSpalatro
98,877

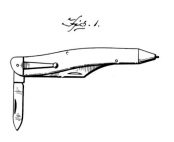

Fig.1.

Fig.2.

Fig.3.

**COMBINED KNIFE AND
PENCIL**
February 22, 1944
Carl Liukko
137,339

**COMBINATION DESK
UNIT**
June 2, 1942
Jacques Martial
132,638

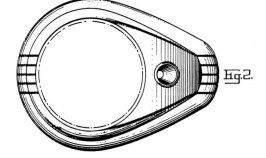

Fig.2.

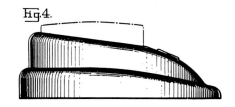

Fig.4.

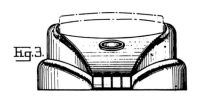

Fig.3.

DUPLICATING MACHINE

October 3, 1939

Willis A. Kropp

116,935

CHECK WRITING MACHINE

August 28, 1934

Henry Dreyfuss

Walter B. Payne

93,157

Henry Dreyfuss's and Walter Payne's 1934 check writer, the Todd "Protectograph" (Des. 93,157), and Willis Kropp's 1939 duplicating machine (Des. 116,935) are examples of what Dreyfuss called "cleanlining"—pared-down revisions of the old sleeve-catchers of the decade before. While the basic arrangement of parts and functions was retained, the machines were given a simplified shell that concealed their most inhospitable parts.

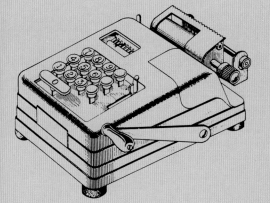

COMPUTING AND LISTING MACHINE

February 13, 1940

Louis M. Llorens

118,962

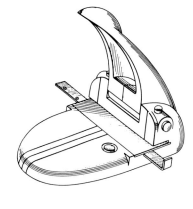

PUNCH

July 7, 1942

Robert Davol Budlong

132,970

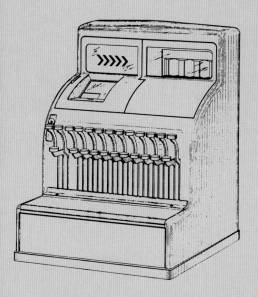

CASH REGISTER

March 21, 1939

Walter D. Teague

Walter D. Teague, Jr.

Edward W. Herman

113,900

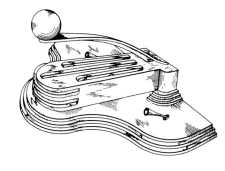

COMBINATION STAPLING MACHINE AND DESK UNIT

August 3, 1937

Roy E. Peterson

105,499

TAPE DISPENSER

April 22, 1941

Jean Otis Reinecke

126,733

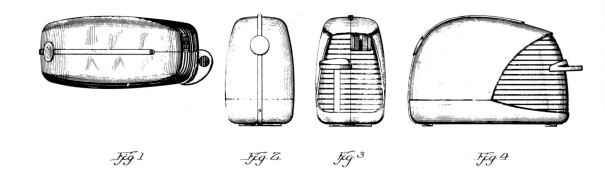

The plastic shell of a Scotch Tape dispenser is as taken for granted now as the curved ends of a paper clip, but like many items it had its origins in the mind of a designer looking for the most obvious form. Jean Reinecke was contracted by Scotch Tape to create a simple, functional dispenser, and thus arrived at one of the most successful and ubiquitous examples of 20th century packaging (Des. 118,629).

TAPE DISPENSER

January 23, 1940

Jean Otis Reinecke

118,629

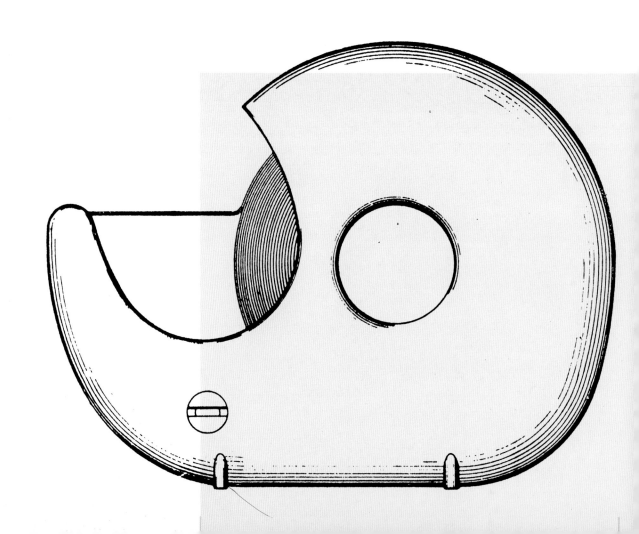

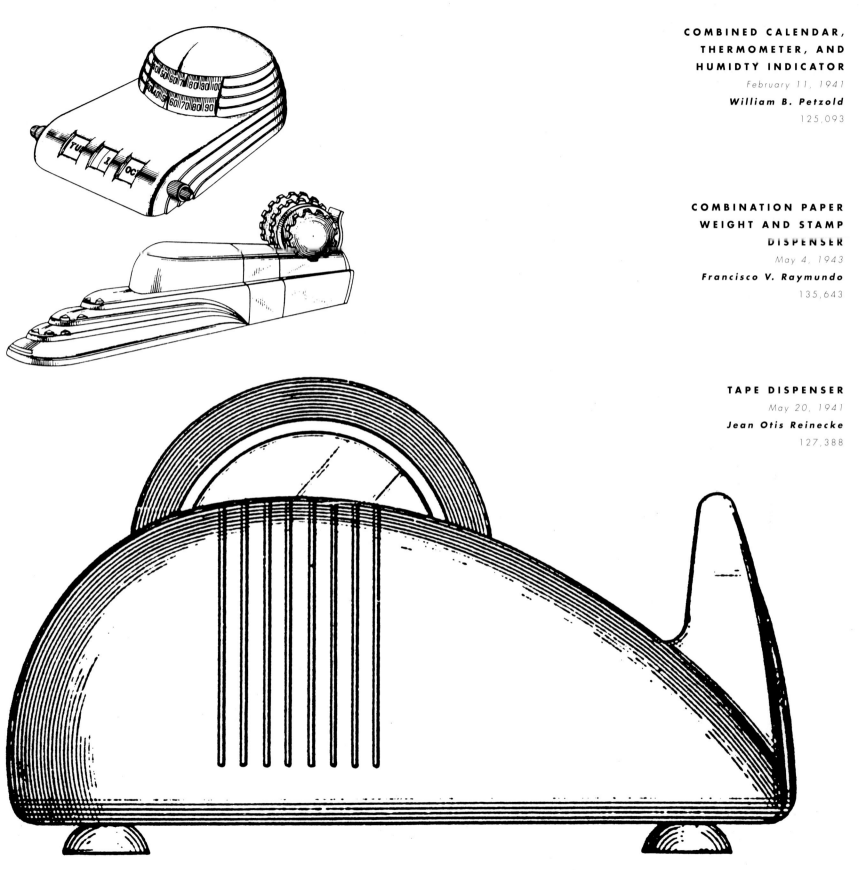

**COMBINED CALENDAR,
THERMOMETER, AND
HUMIDTY INDICATOR**
February 11, 1941
William B. Petzold
125,093

**COMBINATION PAPER
WEIGHT AND STAMP
DISPENSER**
May 4, 1943
Francisco V. Raymundo
135,643

TAPE DISPENSER
May 20, 1941
Jean Otis Reinecke
127,388

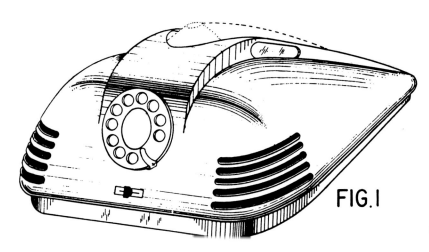

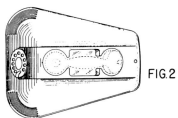

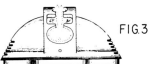

FIG.2

FIG.3

FIG.1

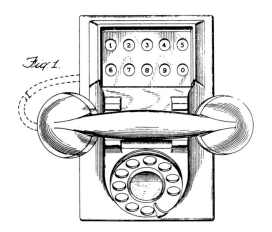

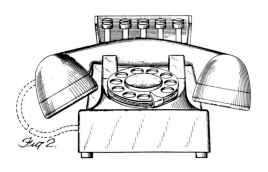

LOUD-SPEAKING TELEPHONE SET
April 13, 1943
Gabriel M. Giannini
135,495

Obergfell's burly telephone desk stand (Des. 117,876) looks like a piece of 1930s road construction. Giannini's loud-speaking telephone set (Des. 135,495) has the low, curving profile of a racing machine about to take off. Both reflect the designer's growing involvement with the form of an increasingly crucial appliance. The telephone set, like many other machines that eventually became standard fare, was first conceived in countless variations.

TELEPHONE DESK STAND
November 28, 1939
Herbert F. Obergfell
117,876

LOUD-SPEAKING TELEPHONE
March 30, 1943
Gabriel M. Giannini
135,389

COMBINED TELEPHONE DESK STAND AND HAND SET
April 17, 1945
Gerald Deakin
140,904

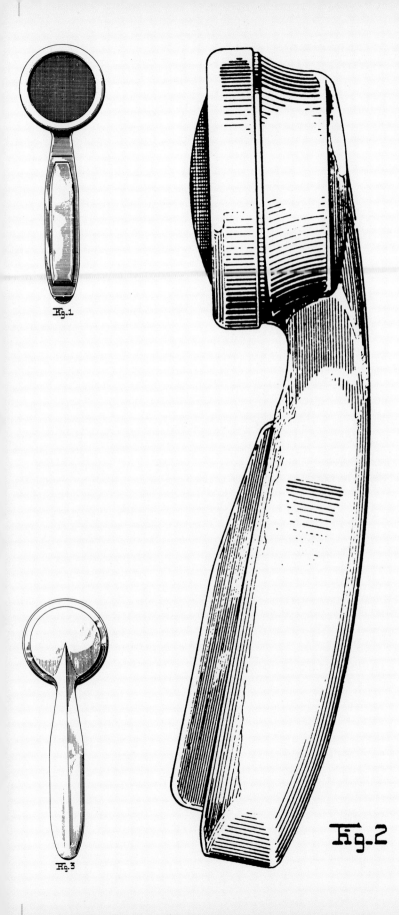

Fig.1

Fig.2

Fig.3

HAND MICROPHONE

March 27, 1945

Gustav F. Braun

140,684

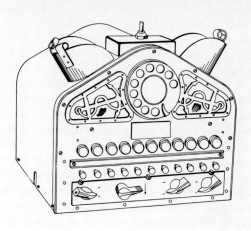

LOUD SPEAKING
TELEPHONE DESK SET
June 5, 1945
Theodore C. Riebe
141,511

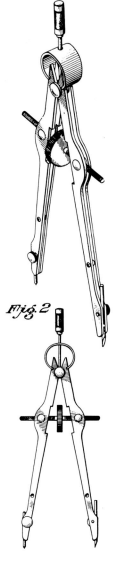

"Today the convenience of phones is established, and they occupy the most accessible place in the home or office or store. Twenty-five years ago some people weren't quite sure where to put them. They were sometimes kept inside plaster globes of the world or cabinets or dolls with fluffy skirts."—*Henry Dreyfuss, 1952*

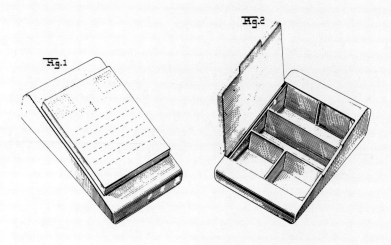

COMBINED CALENDAR
PAD AND DESK
RECEPTACLE
January 7, 1941
Gustav Jensen
124,531

CASING FOR A
TELEPHONE INDEX OR
LIKE ARTICLE
January 30, 1934
Norman Bel Geddes
Worthen Paxton
91,416

COMPASS
March 2, 1943
Floyd G. Eubanks
135,138

STOOL

June 17, 1941

Lawrence M. Michelson

127,810

TELEPHONE OPERATOR'S CHAIR

March 30, 1943

W. W. Brown

135,334

CHAIR

April 25, 1939

Albert J. Berna

114,435

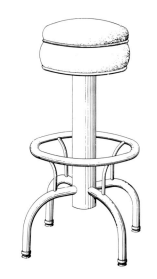

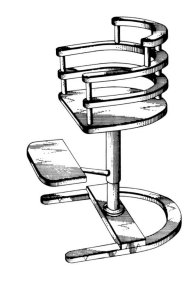

FIG. 1.

FIG. 2.

FIG. 3.

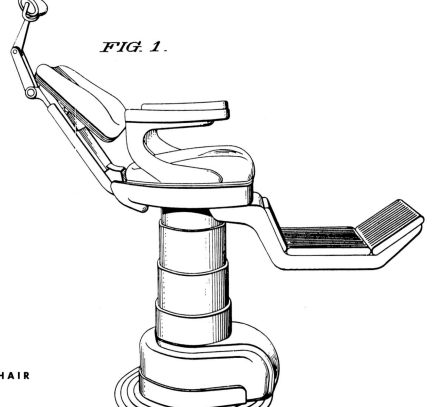

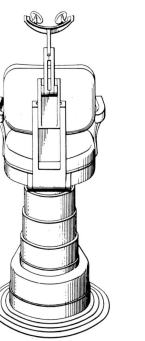

ADJUSTABLE CHAIR

May 26, 1942

Henry Dreyfuss

132,542

FITTING STOOL
February 11, 1936
Wolfgang Hoffman
98,519

Fig. 4

Fig. 3

Fig. 2

Fig. 1

BARBER CHAIR
June 2, 1942
F.J. Piotraschke
132,598

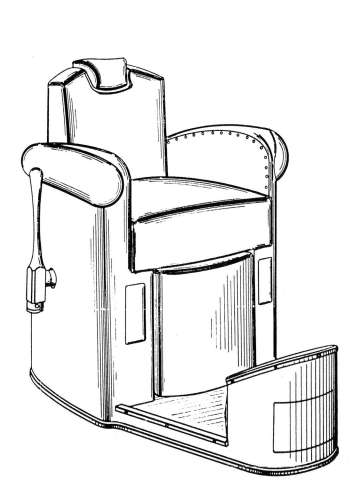

CHAIR

June 29, 1937

Willard H. Bond, Jr.

105,084

The movie theaters of the 1930s were far swankier than the ornate, encrusted picture palaces of the decade before. Their architecture and fittings epitomized the modern elegance of Hollywood's finest: the swells and the toughs, the molls and the angels. An audience could settle into the streamlined chairs (Des. 105,084) with their understated aisle lights and watch Fred Astaire leaping the span of a glossy floor—all black—in a nightclub adorned with machine-age gems. What a way to escape the ragged years of the Depression.

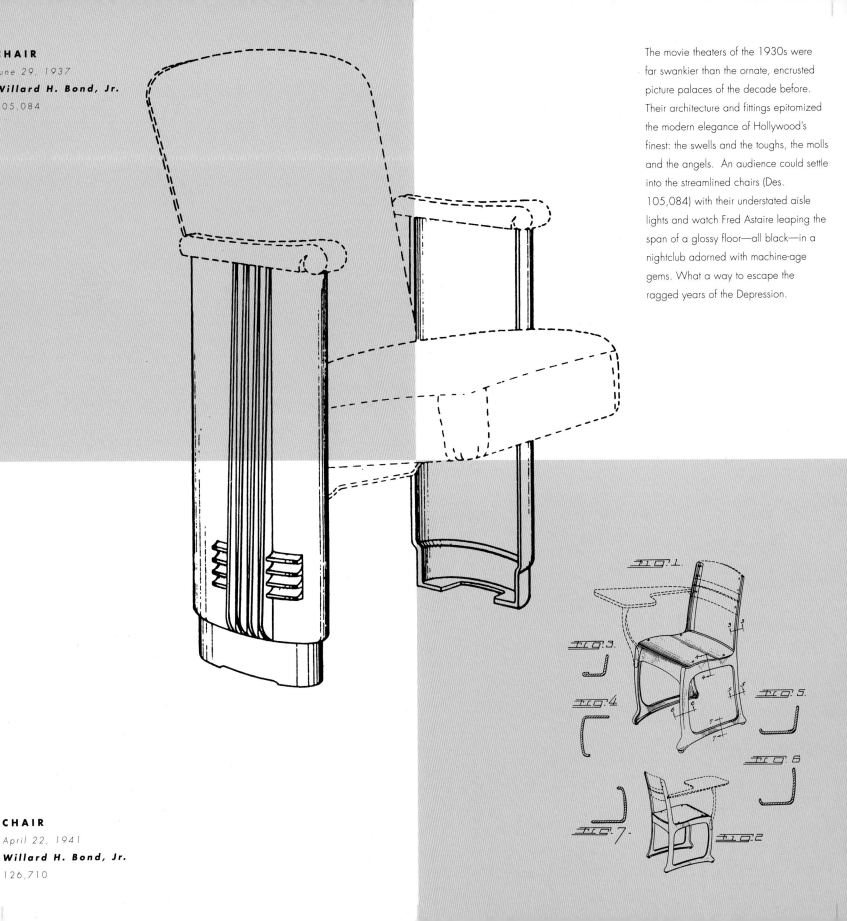

CHAIR

April 22, 1941

Willard H. Bond, Jr.

126,710

GAS MASK

February 25, 1941

William P. Yant

125,486, 125,485

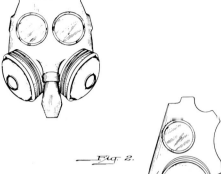

Fig. 1.

Fig. 2.

Fig. 1.

Fig. 2.

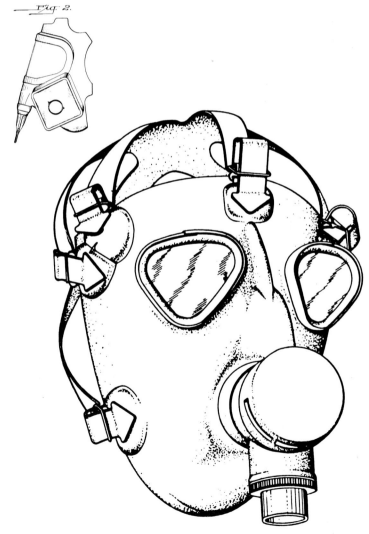

GAS MASK

April 13, 1937

Edward W. Bullard

104,061

In the ten short years since KDKA of Pittsburgh first broadcast the election night returns in 1920, the number of radio-owning families soared. There were 60,000 in 1922; 13,750,000 in 1930. Radio sales, below $2 million in 1920—when large scale manufacturing first began—topped $600 million by 1929. What had started as a static-filled recitation of the evening's headlines was transformed into escape route, entertainer, church, dance hall, comic strip, morale-booster, and newscast. Many would have preferred to maintain the non-commercial sanctity of a straight news broadcast, but advertisers were quick to cash in on radio's potential. Soon not a program or a station was free of a sponsor. Stores and companies flooded the airwaves with cheerful pitches for their wares. ¶ During the hard-luck 1930s the radio got Americans' minds off their troubles, if only for the few hours of an evening's schedule. By 1938 there were four networks—NBC's Red and Blue, CBS, and MBS. On Tuesday, June 7, 1938, NBC's Red station broadcast *Amos n' Andy* at 7, *By Candelight* at 7:30, *Russ Morgan and his Orchestra* on *Jack Johnstone's "Thrill of the Week"* at 8, *The Lady Esther Serenade with Wayne King's Orchestra* at 8:30, and *Fibber McGee and Molly* at 9:30. *Robert Ripley's Believe it or Not* came on at 10, followed by the ever-popular *Jimmie Fidler's Hollywood Gossip*—sure to be filled with the latest on the making of movie blockbusters like *Gone With the Wind*, and occupied at that time with the grandiose search for an actress to play Scarlett O'Hara. ¶ The radio manufacturers had their own sponsors, such as Charlie McCarthy, whose plastic likeness graced the front of a Majestic model, and their own range of styles, from the dignified wooden console—high-priced at fifty dollars and massive as an armchair—to a lipstick-colored table model for fifteen dollars. Plastics made such a cornucopia possible. After the first plastic-encased radio was manufactured in 1931, Bakelite, Catelin, Casein, and Urea became the materials of modern choice. Their compression-molding capabilities enabled designers to create the variety of shapes the manufacturers wanted and gave inventors some zany inspirations. ¶ To hear a silky-voiced announcer describe the outfits of the nightclub swells became a ritual of escapism for some, imitated at home in the ritual of cocktails—which had first entered the cloistered comforts of a living room home during prohibition, bringing with it a wave of stylish accessories like cocktail smokers, streamlined pipes, and novelty ashtrays. Others chose a different set of accessories. By the 1930s photography had reached a point of rapid advancement, with invention following invention and camera manufacturers scrambling to purvey the latest to a buying public made up of as many serious hobbists as Sunday snapshot amateurs. By 1941 there were more than 6,000 camera clubs across the country, averaging 50 or 60 members apiece, and all in the market for the best equipment they could afford. Industrial

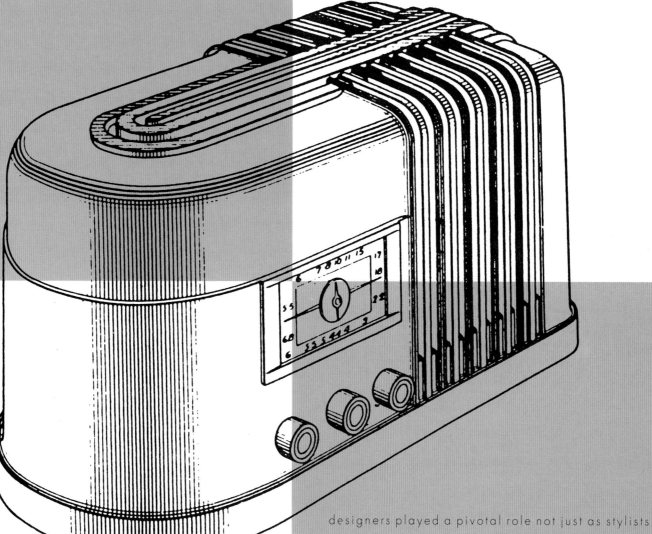

designers played a pivotal role not just as stylists but as inventors too: the teams of Walter Dorwin Teague and Chester Crumrine, and Teague and Joseph Mihalyi, working for Eastman Kodak, produced wonders of mechanics and form like the Bantam Special, a streamlined jewel.

CABINET FOR RADIO RECEIVERS

February 24, 1931

John Geloso

83,436

RADIO RECEIVER CABINET

January 24, 1939

Clarence Karstadt

113,004

RADIO RECEIVER CABINET

April 20, 1937

John R. Morgan

104,197

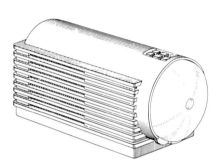

RADIO CABINET

October 10, 1939

Norman Bel Geddes

117,117

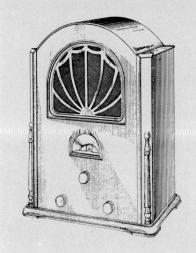

RADIO CABINET

June 2, 1931

Gertrude E. Thompson

84,309

RADIO CABINET

October 10, 1939

Norman Bel Geddes

117,116

RADIO CABINET OR SIMILAR ARTICLE

March 31, 1936

Gail Vandenbraak

99,148

RADIO CABINET

June 23, 1936

Robert Z. Snyder

100,129

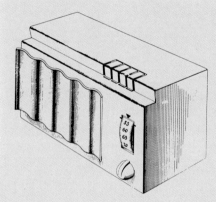

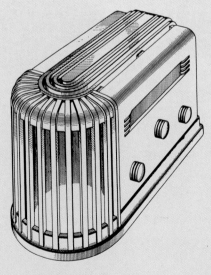

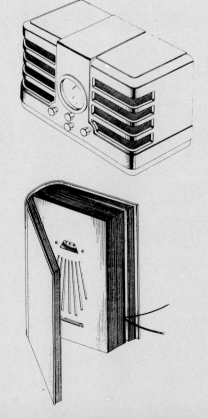

Radios came in endless varieties in the 30s and 40s, from the dignified wooden console to the inventors' favorite singing lamp. A machine age classic, Clarence Karstadt's Model 6110 of 1939 (Des. 113,004) was manufactured by Sears, Roebuck Company and aptly (Sears hoped) named the Silvertone. Other radios advertised high quality fidelity in their shape itself. For parlor-live sound, there was the 1940 Continental (Des. 126,461), a wooden and plastic miniature concert grand with dials and speaker located under the lid. For mellifluous tones there was Kate Lerman's Melody Cruiser (Des. 115,413), manufactured by Majestic with gleaming chrome sails and rigging.

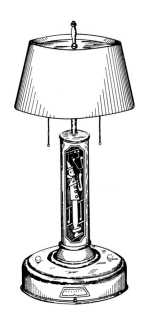

COMBINED LAMP AND
RADIO RECEIVING SET

March 2, 1937

Daniel J. Crowley

103,448

RADIO OR SIMILAR
ARTICLE

June 27, 1939

Kate Lerman

115,413

COMBINED LAMP AND
RADIO RECEIVING SET

August 1, 1939

Daniel J. Crowley

115,953

RADIO CABINET OR THE
LIKE

April 8, 1941

Lester K. Franklin

126,461

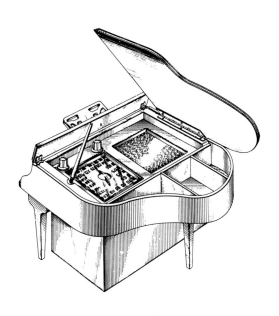

PHONOGRAPH

February 15, 1938

David C. Rockola

108,499

CABINET FOR SOUND REPRODUCING APPARATUS

June 24, 1941

David C. Rockola

127,924

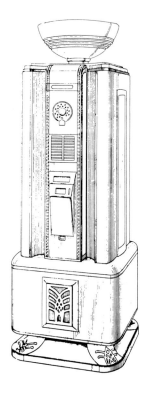

The jukebox owes much to Canadian-born David Rockola, an inventor and entrepreneur who started out in weighing machines and parking meter housings. After he lost money in the coin-operated amusement games business, he needed a scheme to appease angry creditors. In 1930 he convinced them to help him buy old jukebox patents and begin designing his own. Among the masterpieces that put him in competition with the two largest manufacturers, Wurlitzer and Seeburg, was the 1941 dial-a-song Spectravox (Des. 127,924), a wood-grained column with red neon bands and a deflector bowl over the speaker. It was connected to a separate record player, the Playmaster, usually kept hidden behind the bar.

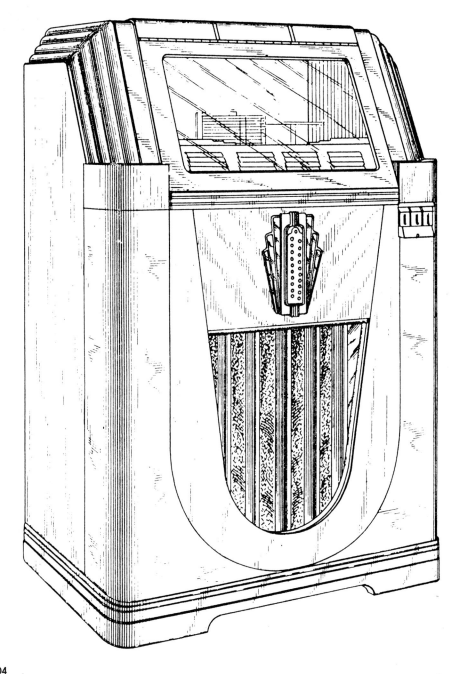

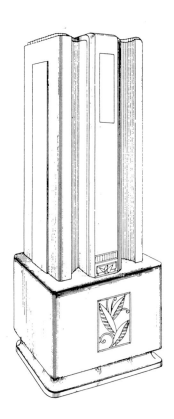

CASING FOR SOUND APPARATUS

October 7, 1941

David C. Rockola

129,860

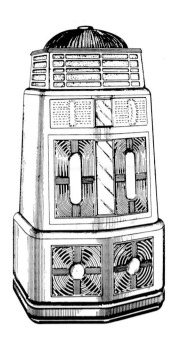

PHONOGRAPH CABINET

June 9, 1942

Henry T. Roberts

132,724

**REMOTE CONTROL
SELECTOR CASING**

October 13, 1936

Lloyd J. Andres

101,576

In 1927 Automatic Musical Instruments was the first company to come out with an electrically amplified phonograph that played multiple selections. Later, in 1939, AMI introduced the first double-sided player—the glass and mottled Bakelite Singing Tower (Des. 132,724). Suddenly the public had not ten, but twenty songs to choose from. Sound poured out of its innovative, horizontally-mounted top speaker, bounced off the glass dome, and hit the room with the impact of a live orchestra.

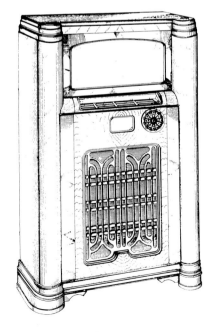

PHONOGRAPH CABINET

June 9, 1936

Paul M. Fuller

99,936

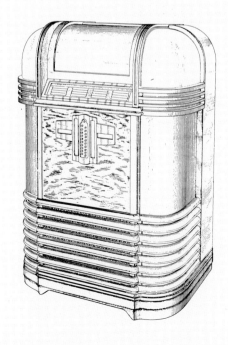

PHONOGRAPH CABINET

February 7, 1939

David C. Rockola

113, 287

Walter Dorwin Teague's collaboration with Kodak produced the 1936 Kodak Bantam Special (Des. 99,906), the first superdeluxe American miniature camera on the market. With its bellows collapsed and its front lid closed, it turned into a streamlined Bakelite shell, stylish and pocket-sized, though at $120 it was too expensive to gain widespread popularity. Teague's 1941 Kodak Medalist (Des. 130,202) featured the latest in larger format technology but was built like a tank, too heavy for fast work. It suffered from Kodak's practice of having engineers, not photographers, invent cameras.

In 1939 location and studio professionals could supply their clients with top-quality color by using the Curtis 3-Color camera (Des. 115,165), which contained interior mirrors that exposed three films simultaneously to produce a color negative. And serious enthusiasts

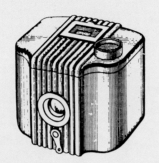

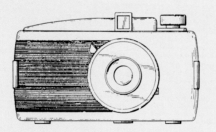

CAMERA

April 18, 1939

Jack Galter

114,324

CAMERA CASING

July 17, 1934

Walter D. Teague

92,830

CAMERA

February 7, 1939

Henry T. Schiff

113,239

CAMERA

November 21, 1939

Henry T. Schiff

117,677

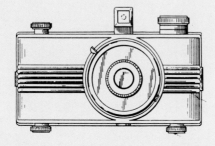

CAMERA

October 28, 1941

Joseph Mihalyi

Walter D. Teague

130,202

CAMERA OR SIMILAR ARTICLE

June 20, 1934

Benjamin Helzick

115,313

CAMERA

June 2, 1936

Walter D. Teague

Chester W. Crumrine

99,906

found an alternative to the popular Speed Graphic in Burke & James's all-metal, 4 x 5 Press Camera of 1941 (Des. 130,120), which sold without lenses for $49.95—half the rival's price. Another B & J line, Watson, offered an Albert Drucker–designed, 5 x 7 view camera (Des. 127,630) whose basic chassis sold for $30. But it was Drucker's Solar Enlarger—a classic still available—that brought B & J fame.

On the other side of the spectrum were cameras for the Sunday snapshot market: the under $10 Spartus (Des. 113,239 and 117,677) and the winning $12.50, 35mm Argus-A (Des. 114,324)—made by a Michigan radio firm, the International Research Corporation, that renamed itself Argus in honor of its bestselling product. The $14.95 Falcon Flash (Des. 115,313) combined flash and camera in one housing—a Depression-era point-and-shoot.

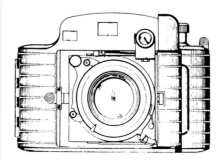

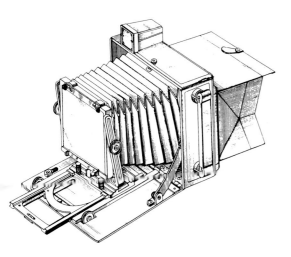

CAMERA

October 28, 1941

Harry S. Drucker

130,120

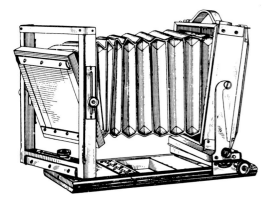

CAMERA

June 3, 1941

Albert Drucker

127,630

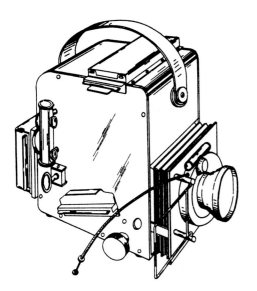

COLOR CAMERA

June 6, 1939

Thomas S. Curtis

115,165

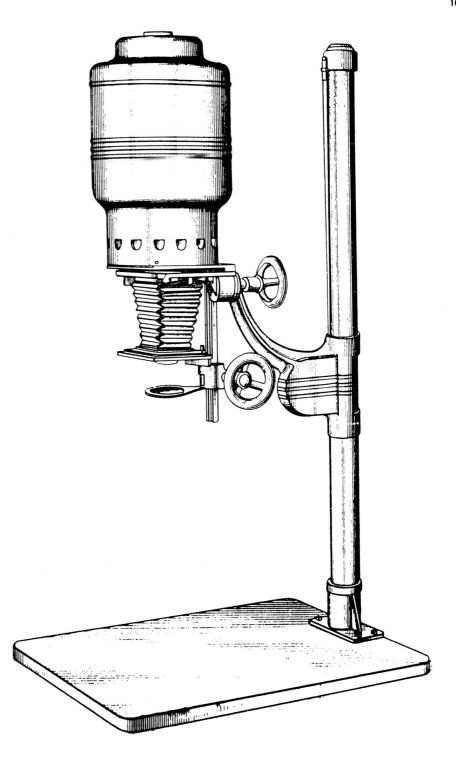

**PHOTOGRAPHIC
ENLARGING APPARATUS**

June 17, 1941

Albert Drucker

127,839

ASHTRAY

February 27, 1940

J.P. Sandejas

119,206

Fig. 1

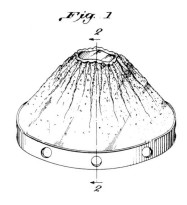

Fig. 2

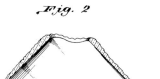

COMBINED CIGARETTE RECEPTACLE AND MATCH HOLDER

January 29, 1935

Evelyn Jahncke

94,424

Fig.1

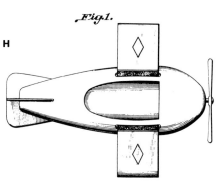

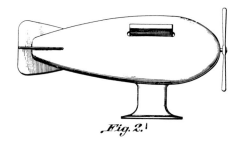

Fig.2.

ASH TRAY

June 16, 1931

Silas J. Hudson

Lawrence M. Gilley

84,416

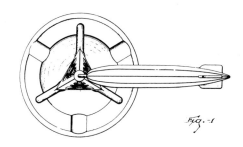

Fig.-1

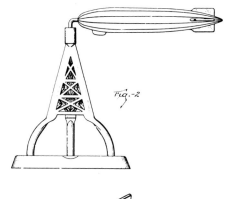

Fig.-2

MATCH FOLDER

January 19, 1937

John H. Lewis

102,856

Fig. 1.

Fig. 2.

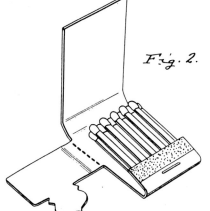

COMBINED ASH TRAY AND STATUETTE

June 6, 1944

Ronald K. Pohl

138,059

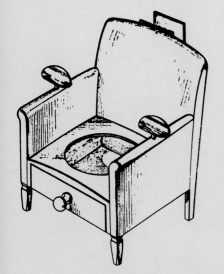

COMBINATION ASH TRAY AND STAND FOR SMOKER'S ARTICLES

February 2, 1932

Vincent Vanshura

86,149

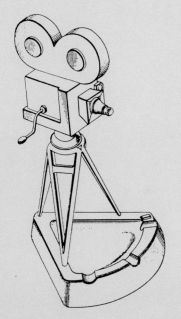

COMBINATION ASH TRAY AND LIGHTER

January 28, 1936

William A. Inglis
Edwin E. Bathke

98,328

"In the design area you have to be really careful, because you can get something that's really suggestive—connoting some sexual impropriety or racial slur. And if you're not astute enough to read into what the person is doing, you're going to grant a design patent that's going to be embarrassing. If the federal government or the climate of the country is accepting of such behavior, then that type of design will occur. But today, we have a different climate."
—*Wallace Burke,*
U.S. Patent and Trademark Office

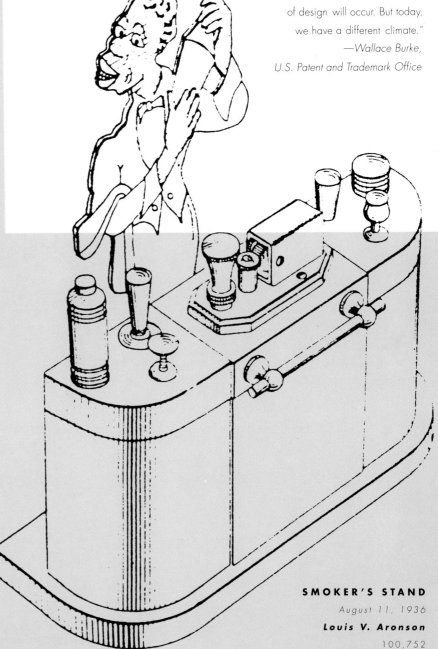

SMOKER'S STAND

August 11, 1936

Louis V. Aronson

100,752

**AIR FINNED SMOKING
PIPE**

May 20, 1941

Wayne Leser

127,324

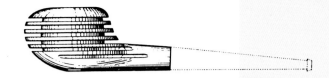

SMOKING PIPE

October 31, 1939

Warren Fuhrman

117,395

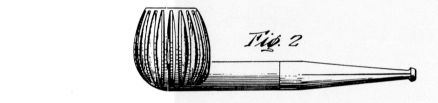

TOBACCO PIPE

November 18, 1941

Arthur E. Desjarlais

130,431

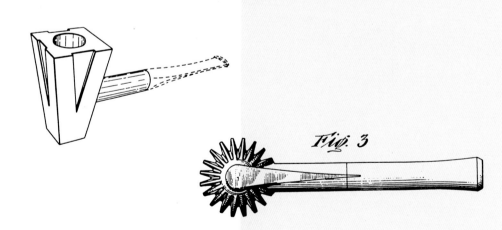

PIPE

September 5, 1939

Jack Galter

116,494

110

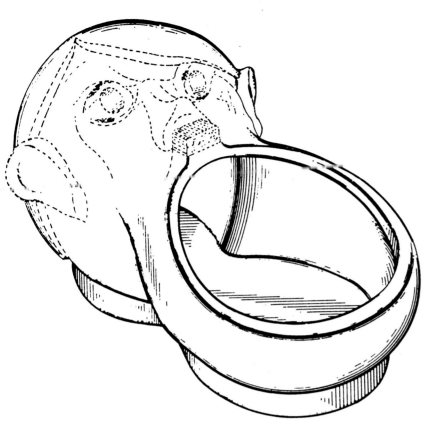

ASH TRAY OR SIMILAR ARTICLE

January 26, 1943

Edward Grossman

134,904

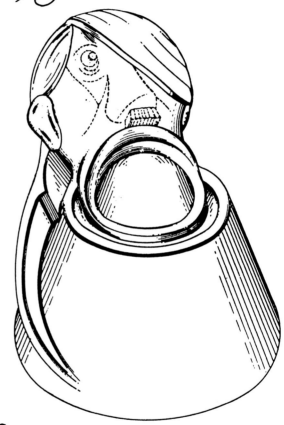

"Design applications which disclose subject matter which could be deemed offensive to any race, religion, sex, ethnic group, or nationality, such as those which include caricatures or depictions, should be rejected as not meeting the requirements of ornamentality . . ."
—Manual of Patent Examining Procedure, U.S. Patent and Trademark Office

Fig.1.

CUSPIDOR OR SIMILAR ARTICLE

October 27, 1942

Edward Grossman

134,162

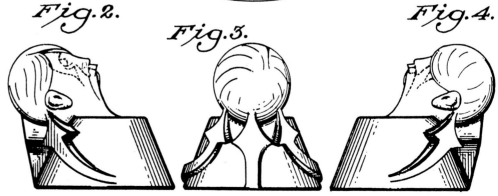

Fig.2.　　*Fig.3.*　　*Fig.4.*

The cocktails-and-cigarettes rite had its classier practitioners, including the Viennese Wolfgang Hoffman, one of many designers who had taken a place among the European avant-garde and, after coming to the United States, made invaluable contributions to American design. His smoking stands, of chrome-plated, tubular steel, were monuments to the machine age and irrepressibly stylish.

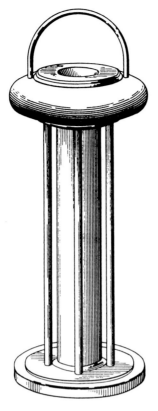

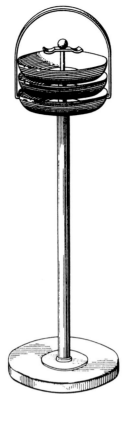

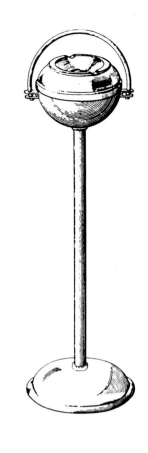

SMOKING STAND

October 6, 1936

Wolfgang Hoffman

101,457, 101,460

SMOKING STAND

January 8, 1935

Wolfgang Hoffman

94,306, 94,307

SMOKING STAND

February 26, 1935

Wolfgang Hoffman

94,690

SMOKING STAND

January 8, 1935

Wolfgang Hoffman

94,308

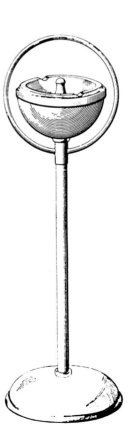

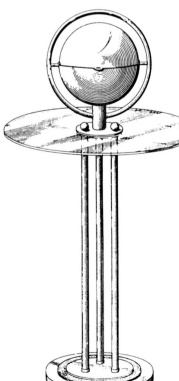

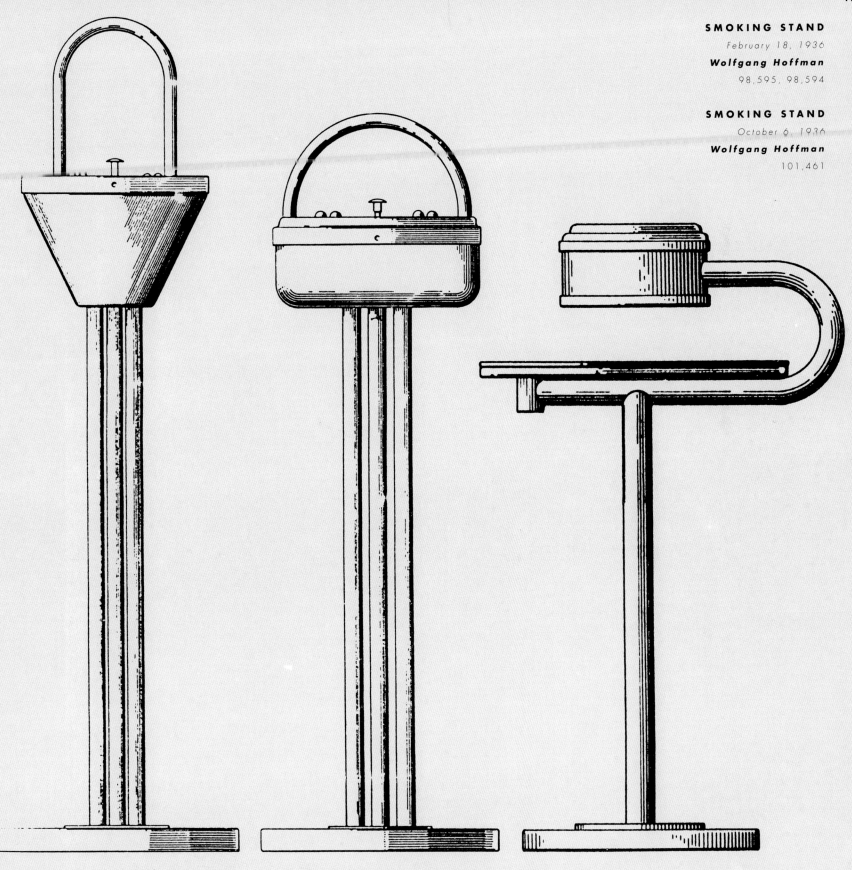

SMOKING STAND
February 18, 1936
Wolfgang Hoffman
98,595, 98,594

SMOKING STAND
October 6, 1936
Wolfgang Hoffman
101,461

For children, the machine age was a time of space-age rocketships blasting off to Planet Mongo, of bicycles so streamlined that a ride down the street was guaranteed to break the land-speed record. Leaning forward and pedaling furiously, head into the wind, the proud owner of a deluxe model Schwinn could feel the balloon tires just about to leave the ground, lifting off on a trans-oceanic journey.

of a robot changing lightbulbs. But his daughter might go up to get a closer look. Some scientific projections spent the long wait for adult use as tin toys in the playroom. ¶ But the giant steps made in mechanical production during the machine age enabled even the smallest items to become gimmicks. Borden's, Horton's, and Reed's were all licensed to make Mel-o-rolls—cylinders of chocolate, vanilla,

toys & playthings

Just in case there was any trouble along the way, a trusty Buck Rogers rocket gun would blast the enemies into invisible matter to be borne back to their evil planets by reverse gravity. ¶ Crossing the boundary between fact and fantasy was no issue for the inventors and designers working in the world of play. A child's imagination was the only motor a model truck required, the only engine needed by a coaster wagon with wheels encased in teardrop pontoons, to be transfigured into a racing seaplane. However simple or naive, whatever disregard for mechanics and practical ratios their chassis may have displayed, many toys were the first incarnations of the future. A father at the Westinghouse exhibit at the 1939 New York World's Fair might shake his head when confronted with the concept

and strawberry ice cream each individually wrapped in perforated papers—a cinch for the soda jerk to drop into an ice cream soda or into the specially shaped recess of a patented cone. For the traveling fairs that pitched their tents in small towns, the ready supply of novelty booths meant they could come back again and again with newer, more thrilling, more exciting amusements. To Woolworth's, the manufacturers's steady production of die-cast metal Tootsie Toy cars was vital for maintaining an eager cadre of younger customers. Improvements in production and packaging cast a bright and expansive light on the toy market, but modern design made a bigger difference. Even in toys that hearkened back to their 19th century origins, like the sled and the roller skate, the more streamlined they looked, the better.

TOY GUN

December 15, 1936

Otto A. Langos

102,382

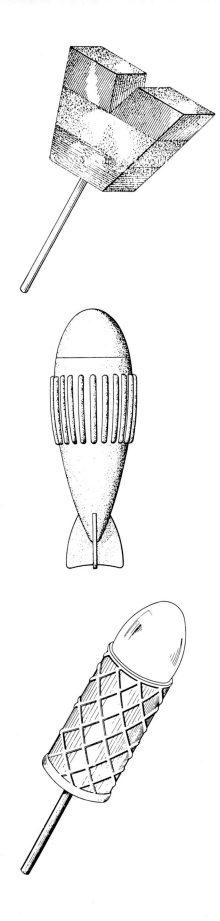

CONFECTION
May 19, 1942
Nicholas S. Sabatino
132,467

ICE CREAM CONE
May 12, 1942
Earl M. James
132,402

Patenting a new design for the ubiquitous ice cream cone is no small accomplishment. However, the novelty was unmistakable in the case of Mr. Houston's cone (Des. 118,624), since it was designed for the 1939 New York World's Fair. Nevertheless, an examiner assigned to handle the classification of such trifles was required by law to make a thorough search—starting with other ice cream cones. As Wallace Burke of the U.S. Patent Office explained, "If we have a design application for a hammer for example, we look in tools. We don't look in jewelry just because the hammer happens to have something that may look like something you saw hanging from someone's ear the other day."

CONFECTION
April 7, 1942
Eugene H. Hale
131,946

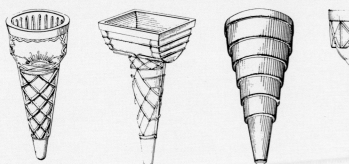

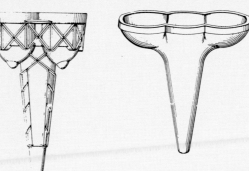

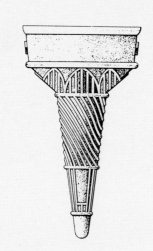

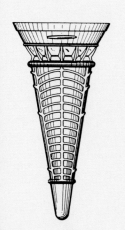

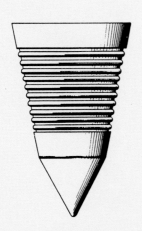

ICE CREAM CONE
September 5, 1933
Sol S. Leaf
90,624

ICE CREAM CONE
April 17, 1934
David Canter
91,982

ICE CREAM CONE
May 15, 1934
Sol S. Leaf
92,261

ICE CREAM CONE
January 2, 1934
Sol S. Leaf
91,274

ICE CREAM CONE
August 7, 1934
Sol S. Leaf
92,967

ICE CREAM CONE
March 10, 1936
James Balton
98,821

ICE CREAM CONE
January 14, 1941
James Balton
124,647, 124,646

ICE CREAM CONE
January 27, 1942
Ernest A. Hamwi
131,221

ICE CREAM CONE
November 7, 1939
B.W. Devereux
117,449

ICE CREAM CONE
January 23, 1940
William A. Houston
118,624

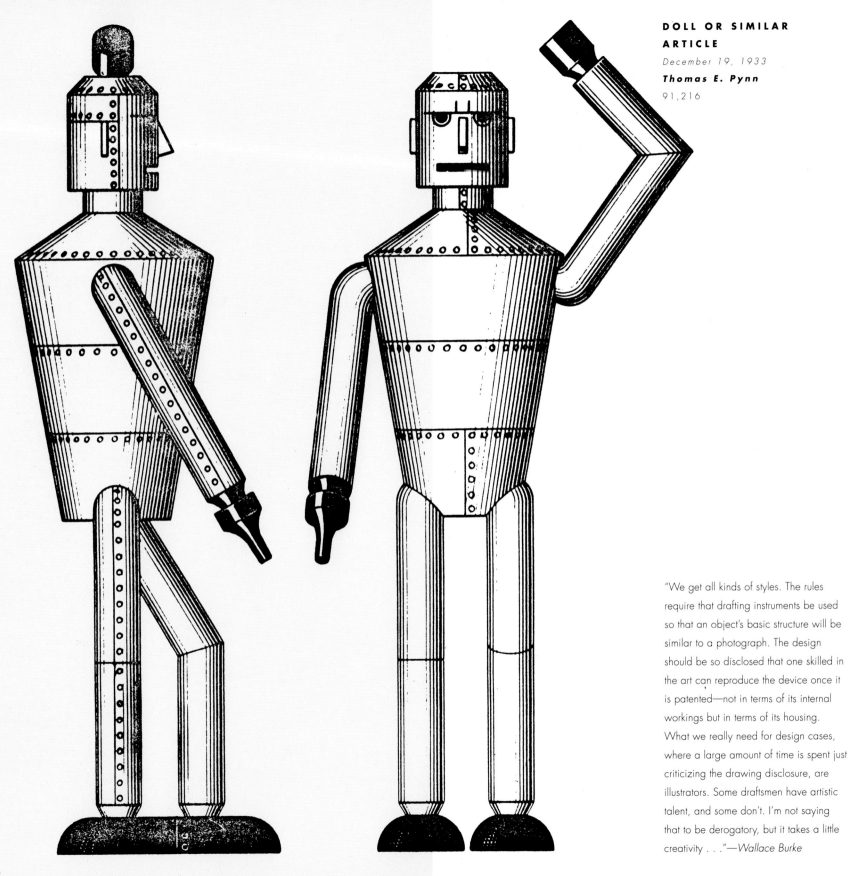

DOLL OR SIMILAR ARTICLE

December 19, 1933

Thomas E. Pynn

91,216

"We get all kinds of styles. The rules require that drafting instruments be used so that an object's basic structure will be similar to a photograph. The design should be so disclosed that one skilled in the art can reproduce the device once it is patented—not in terms of its internal workings but in terms of its housing. What we really need for design cases, where a large amount of time is spent just criticizing the drawing disclosure, are illustrators. Some draftsmen have artistic talent, and some don't. I'm not saying that to be derogatory, but it takes a little creativity . . ."—*Wallace Burke*

MECHANICAL MAN
January 19, 1937
Rafael A.S. Busto
102,815

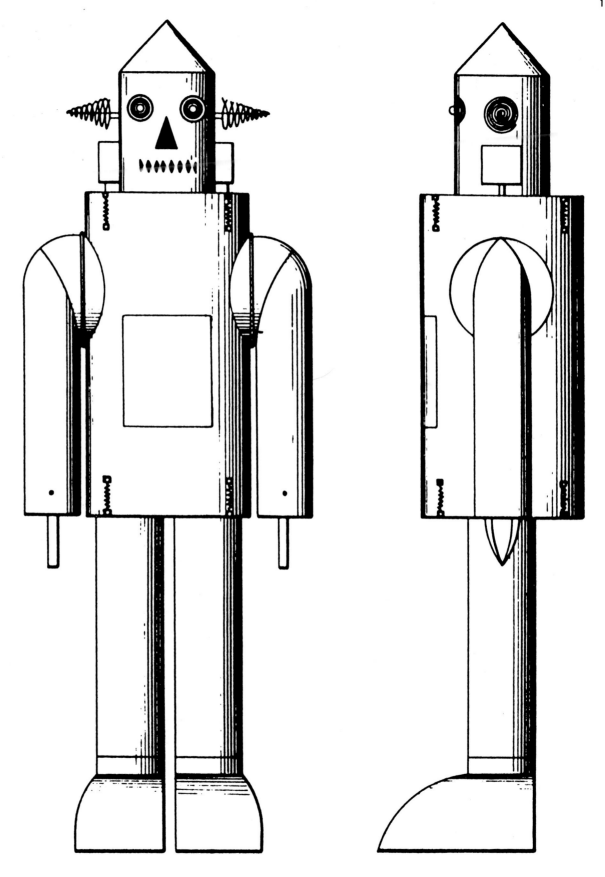

Frank Schwinn set the racy standard for bicycles with swift-looking models like the 1939 Autocycle (Des. 115,942), all arcs and angles on a cantilevered frame. Here was a sturdy fantasy for children—the more curved and gadgeted the better. It came complete with whitewall tires and a shock absorbing seat and was perfect for a child's dream of space travel through Anytown, U.S.A.

BICYCLE

July 11, 1944

Earl S. Boynton

138,304

**ROCKING-HORSE
VELOCIPEDE**

April 8, 1941

Henry Sylvester Schnack

126,371

BICYCLE

February 28, 1939

John Vassos

113,584

VELOCIPEDE

June 24, 1941

E.J. Weller, Jr.

127,915

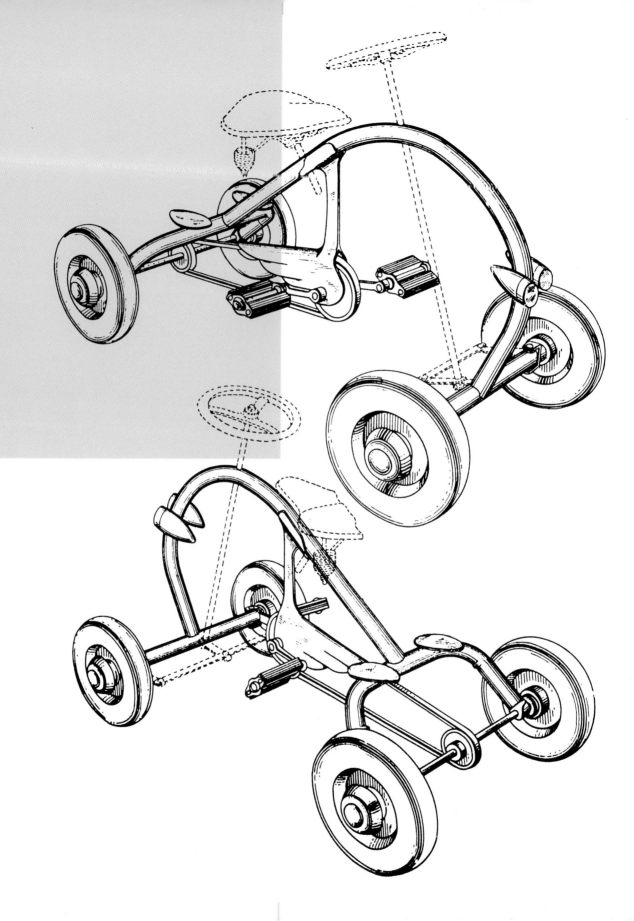

TRICYCLE
June 30, 1936
Harry H. Henry
100,212

Fig.1.

Fig.2.

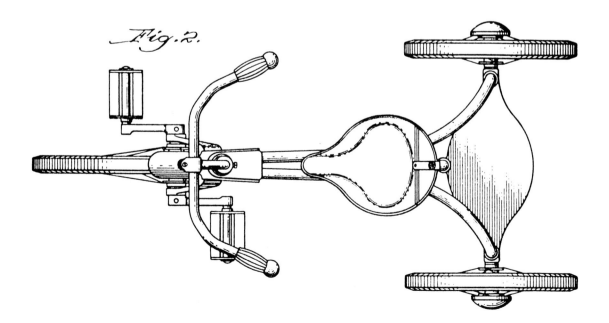

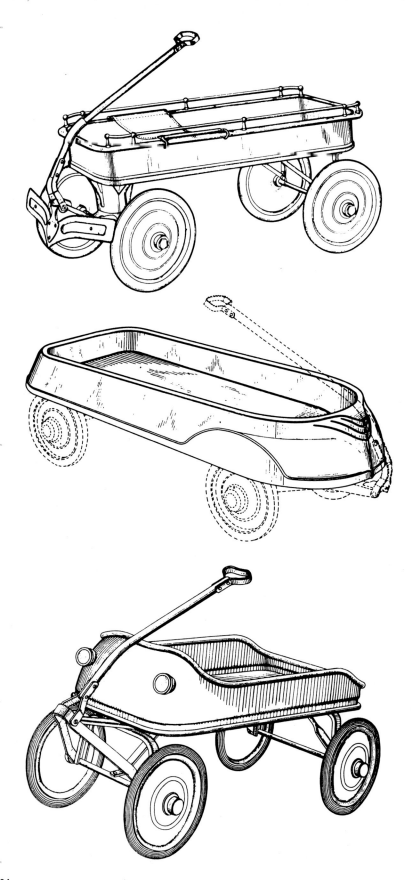

The August 1935 issue of *Modern Mechanix* highlighted a new wagon that was a predecessor of J. B. Eck's 1937 model (Des. 104,678), with the kind of attention usually paid to a new car. "Improved steering is featured on the latest type of streamlined coaster wagon. The handle cannot catch on wagon box and upset the rider. A metal link projects through semi-circular slot in body to connect handle to wheel. Headlights are recessed and even wheels have mudguards."

COASTER WAGON

April 3, 1934

Joseph B. Eck

91,862

COASTER WAGON

May 25, 1937

Joseph B. Eck

104,678

COASTER WAGON

February 20, 1934

Antonio Pasin

91,540

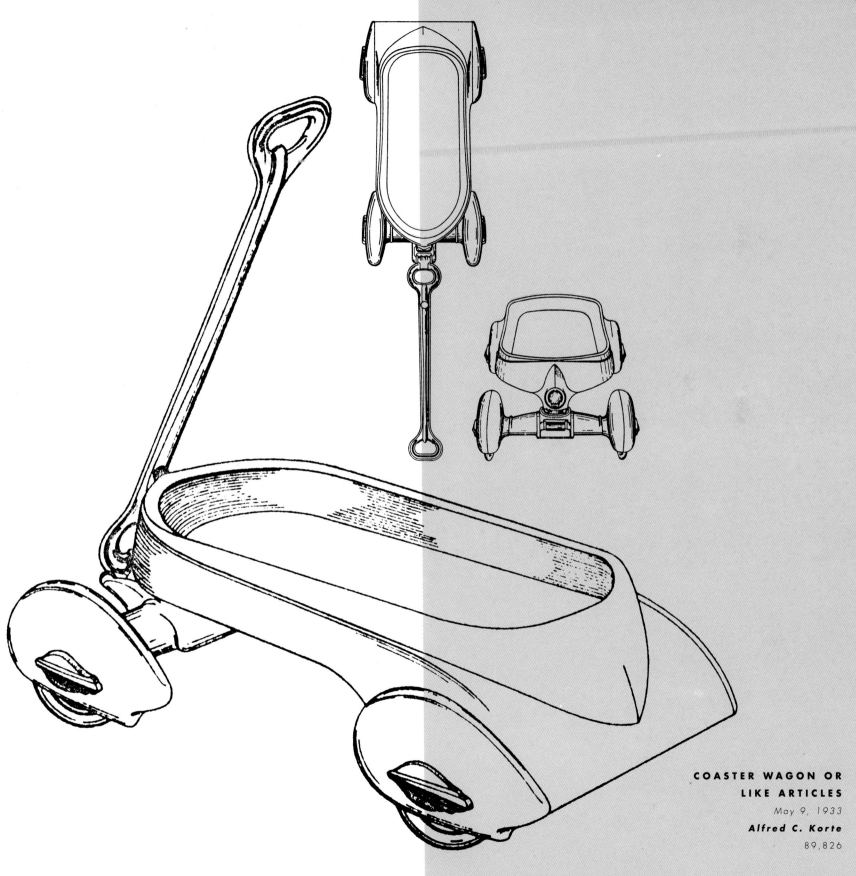

COASTER WAGON OR
LIKE ARTICLES
May 9, 1933
Alfred C. Korte
89,826

CIRCULAR RIDING DEVICE

May 12, 1936

Clifford I. Sweet

99,613

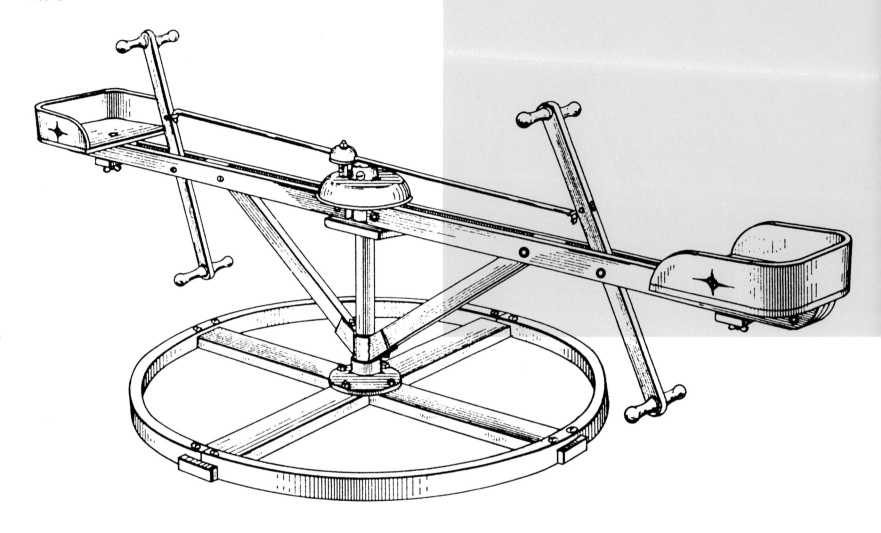

In 1930, a novelty search for a roller skate might take a patent examiner to the 62nd patent classification, which included toys and amusement devices, as well as furniture, fishing and trapping, baggage, and package and article carriers. An examiner might also look in the 41st patent classification, for land vehicles, wheels and axles, resilient tires and wheels, and wheel substitutes; and in the 11th, which included boots, shoes, and harnesses.

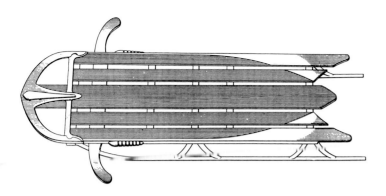

SLED
June 30, 1936
John R. Morgan
100,220

ROLLER SKATE
October 5, 1937
Norman W. Norman
106,323

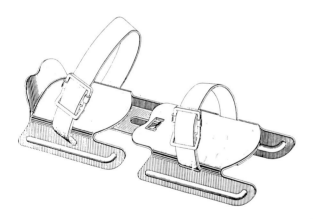

ICE SKATE
October 16, 1934
Ralph P. Hammond
93,618

SELF-PROPELLED SURF BOARD
July 14, 1942
Bert Lee
133,078

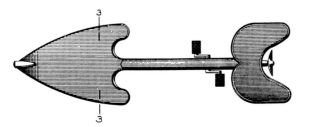

JUVENILE VEHICLE

February 27, 1945

William I. Smith

140,435, 140,434

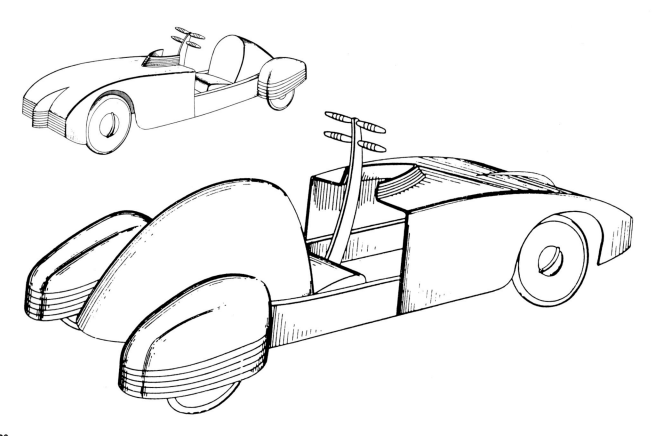

W. I. Smith's kiddie cars had up-to-the-minute contemporary styling. His finned model of 1945 (Des. 140,435) featured the same psychographics as a World War II Flying Tiger fighter plane—a shark's tooth mouth, fierce eyes, and a streamlined propeller.

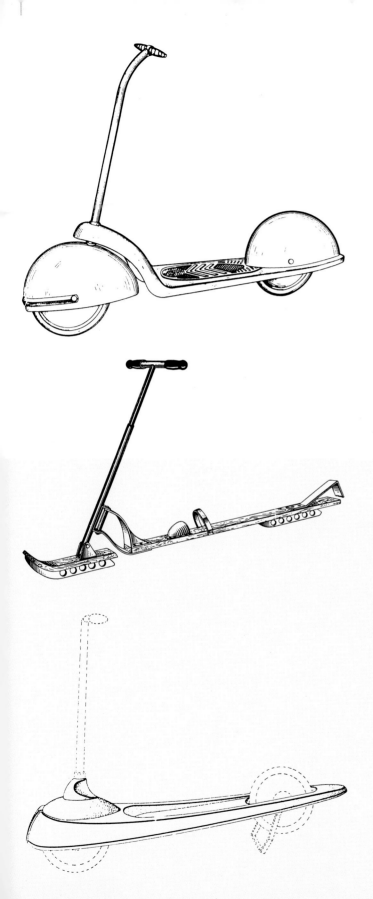

SCOOTER
May 25, 1937
Joseph B. Eck
104,679

SCOOTER SKI
April 29, 1941
Ralph R. Hylan
126,833

SCOOTER
April 7, 1936
Harold L. Van Doren
John G. Rideout
99,225

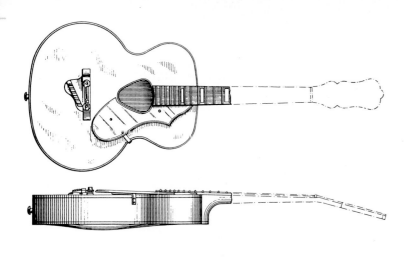

GUITAR OR SIMILAR
MUSICAL INSTRUMENT
September 16, 1941
Fred Gretsch, Jr.
129,478

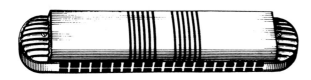

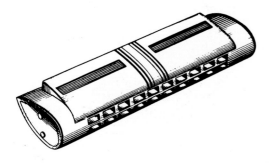

HARMONICA
August 8, 1939
John Vassos
116,068, 116,067

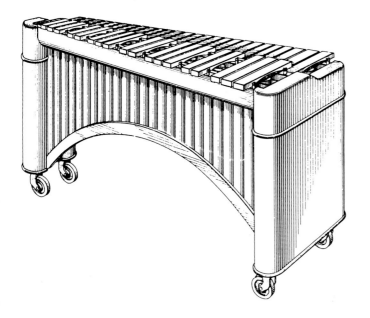

MARIMBA
July 7, 1936
Clair Omar Musser
100,334

**COMBINED PLATFORM
SCALE AND VENDING
DEVICE**
January 24, 1939
Claude R. Kirk
113,006

WEIGHING SCALE
August 1, 1939
Burns S. Watling
115,944

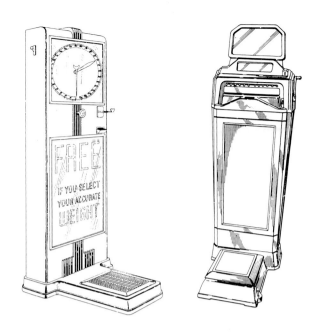

**ASTROLOGICAL AND
MYSTIC ROBOT**
June 13, 1939
Joseph P. Wilson
115,225

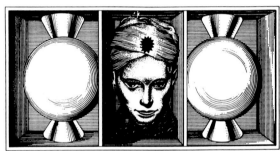

GAME BOARD
May 2, 1939
William A. Fuld
114,534

**MASQUERADE FLYING
SUIT**
December 1, 1936
Michael Couchman
102,204

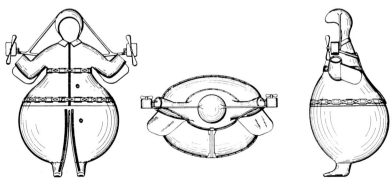

In a drafting studio somewhere in Chicago or Detroit or Washington D.C.—where there's a brisk trade in the patent drawing business—a young apprentice sits at his table perched on his stiff-backed, metal stool, the heels of his scuffed wingtips hooked into the rungs. Before him are a designer's sketches and copious notes for a festive textile pattern, which may be meant for a woman's sundress or skirt since the fabric—in a Hawaiian motif with leis and palm trees—will be bright and cheery. The designer's long list of instructions reads like a vacation brochure itself: background, brilliant azure; orchids, shell pink; leis, fiery orange. There won't be any actual colors in the drawing, but the apprentice will signify them by using the drafting codes he's memorized—slanted lines for one color, dots for another, and dashes for yet another. ¶ As he begins marking up his fresh bristol board for the placement of flowers and hula dancers, the apprentice's mind begins to wander. Outside the big window of the third-floor studio it's getting darker as night settles on the city and a steady October rain runs in currents down the glass. *Some job*, he thinks. Last week he drew a set of sunglasses straight out of Hollywood, the frame trimmed with tropical leaves; before that it was a victory pin. He flicks on the radio for company and Artie Shaw's band fills the room with brassy notes. There might

be a bulletin soon with the latest news from overseas—there's a war on, after all. Now that he's eighteen, his number may come up any day. ¶ The War Production Board's 1942 limits on clothing materials and styles—no frills, no baubles, no nylons (the miracle fiber belongs in parachutes) hasn't stopped the patenting end of the fashion business, though the country's making do as best it can. The magazines are full of ads hailing austerity as an act of patriotism, which it is. As the Pepperell mill points out, "Regular fabrics for civilian needs may be made after—and only after—Task No. 1 is done." Maybe some fabrics won't be made, but they're certainly being designed, and there's plenty to patent for war-time use. The apprentice has found himself working late nights to finish everything from cowboy and Indian scarves to sturdy children's playclothes, and the factory overalls and trousers designed for the women working on the assembly lines during the war. ¶ Some aspects of fashion seem vital despite their apparent frivolity: the stores are full of "furlough nighties." Shoe stylists have been patenting high-heeled, strappy sandals for those Friday night dances at the U.S.O. Raymond Loewy has created a much-heralded cardboard lipstick tube whose style makes up for its impermanence—the metals and plastics it might have been made of have been diverted for use in munitions. Others are applying for patents

fashion&accessories

on designs clearly meant for the victory days ahead: dresses made of yards and yards of cloth, shoes of sumptuous leather. ¶ So the apprentice keeps at the Hawaiian pattern, plotting its riotous shapes. He carefully letters the words *Waikiki*,

Maui, Poi, Paradise. Nice to think about paradise on a rainy night in an empty drafting studio, while the country's in the middle of a war. But in his short year at the drafting firm, he's learned to take his time. Designers may seem rushed, full

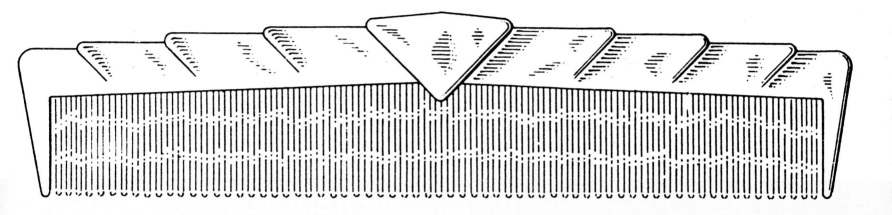

COMB
February 22, 1944
Anthony J. Desimone
137,319

of the urgency of protecting what they've just created. But they'd rather see precision than haste. The risk of rejection is just that much greater if the drawing isn't right, and a small firm like this one that caters to the lone designers and inventors,

and not the big names with their in-house drafting teams, doesn't want to make mistakes. Besides, you never know when you might wind up working on a drawing for something that not only receives a patent, but actually gets manufactured. Maybe it'll be a big hit. Maybe the inventor will strike it rich. ¶ You never know.

FABRIC

January 9, 1945

Arthur Y. Park

139,977, 139,971, 139,979,
139,990

FABRIC

January 16, 1945

Arthur Y. Park

140,043

TEXTILE FABRIC

April 20, 1937

Elsie J. Das

104,133

SANDAL

May 8, 1945

Mollie Gordon

141,114

SHOE

February 11, 1941

Frank R. Merritt

125,090

SHOE

January 14, 1941

Harold L. Pierson

124,611

SHOE OR SIMILAR ARTICLE

September 12, 1939

Oswald M. Pick

116,598

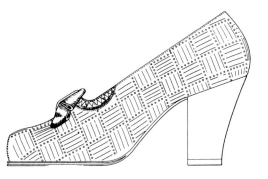

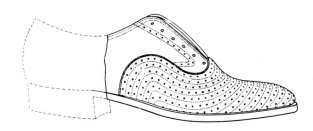

SANDAL

March 10, 1942

Gus E. Bergman

131,587

SHOE

January 14, 1941

Robert S. Cook

124,600

SANDAL OR SIMILAR ARTICLE

May 30, 1939

Herschel S. Davis

115,028

SHOE

March 13, 1945

Jacob Sandler

140,573

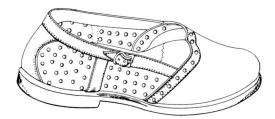

SHOE
October 24, 1939
William F. Cairns
117.330

1932–1934 average prices: Women's leather shoes, $1.79. Men's leather shoes, $3.85. Women's silk stockings, 69¢ a pair. Men's silk necktie, 55¢ each. Women's wool suit, $3.96. Men's wool suit, $10.50. Men's Stetson hat, $5.00.

SHOE
March 10, 1942
Roger Vivier
131.543

Fig.1

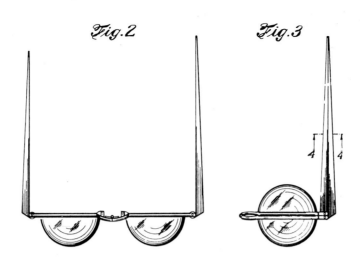

Fig.2   *Fig.3*

Edward McGlynn's 1939 sun goggles
(Des. 114,994) ingeniously folded into
the trylon and perisphere symbol of the
World's Fair.

SUN GOGGLES
May 30, 1939
Edward McGlynn
114,994

SUNGLASSES
August 1, 1939
Jacques E. Maisch
115,933

SPECTACLE FRAME
August 26, 1941
H. King Halikman
129,119

GOGGLE
July 25, 1939
Samuel E. Bouchard
115,877

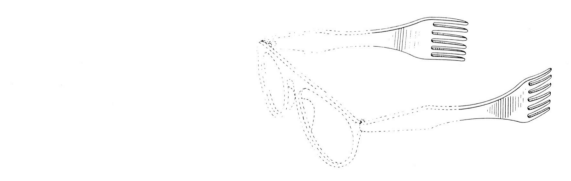

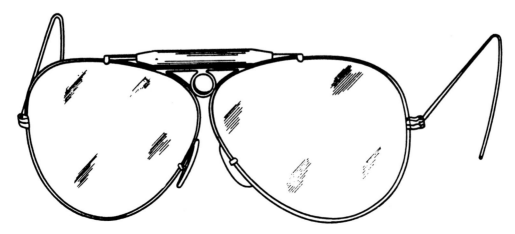

TOOTHBRUSH

January 8, 1935

Walter W. Hadley

94,303

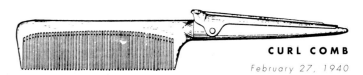

CURL COMB

February 27, 1940

N.L. Solomon

119,219

TOOTHBRUSH

August 5, 1941

Luis L. Reinold

128,681

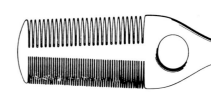

FINGER-GRIP COMB

February 6, 1940

Ethel Yates Berry

118,810

FOUNTAIN TOOTHBRUSH

June 10, 1941

Hyman W. Bergman

127,731

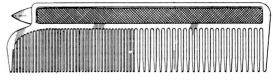

**COMBINATION COMB
AND FINGER NAIL FILE**

April 18, 1944

Robert C. Torian

137,721

The wartime shortages of 1942 caused a surge in advertising based on patriotic duties, including hygienic ones. "Keeping fit is America's duty! Do your part by keeping well," read the ad for Dr. West's Miracle Tuft toothbrushes.

COMB

January 21, 1936

John J. Kohlmeyer

98,257

WATCH FOB PLATE OR SIMILAR ARTICLE

February 11, 1941

Herman Tabor

125,097

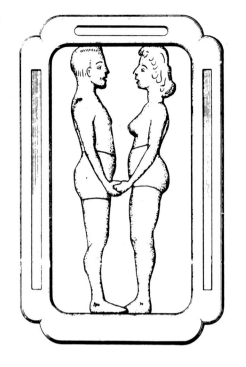

WRIST WATCH

June 21, 1938

Emanuel L. Arzt

110,166

COMBINATION WRIST WATCH AND COMPASS AND STRAP THEREFOR

May 4, 1943

Emil Von Burg

135,635

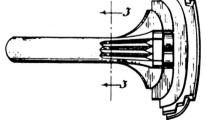

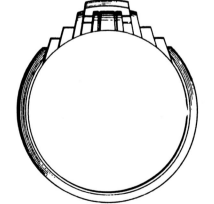

FINGER RING

January 14, 1941

Arthur P. Terryberry

124,659

Fig.1   *Fig.2*   *Fig.3*

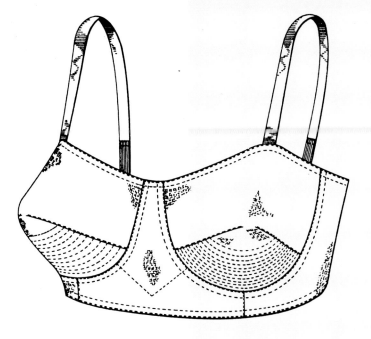

Despite Raymond Loewy's prediction that
women's bodies would progress to
slimmer and slimmer lines just like other
objects (his last sketch in the progression
from bustle inwards is a question mark),
William Rosenthal's brassiere patent of
1937 (Des. 103,068) was made for full
figures, popularized in the mid-1930s
thanks to Mae West.

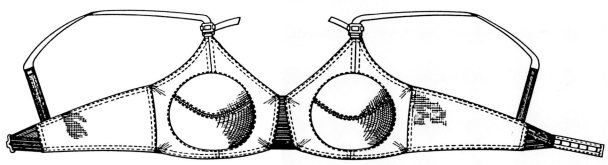

BRASSIERE OR THE LIKE
April 29, 1941
William Rosenthal
126,918

BRASSIERE
January 7, 1936
William Rosenthal
98,090

CAP

January 16, 1945

Paul M. Maxwell
Wilhelmina J. Russy

140,040

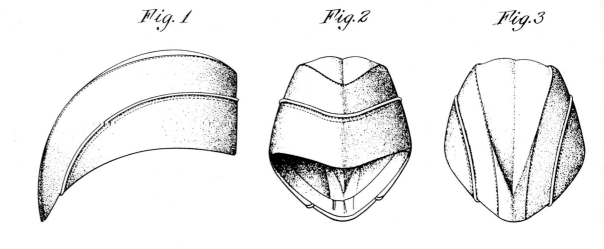

Fig. 1 *Fig. 2* *Fig. 3*

CAP

May 9, 1944

Paul M. Maxwell
Wilhelmina J. Russy

137,892

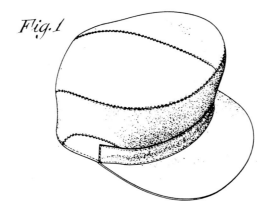
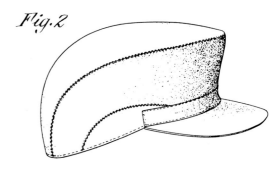

Fig. 1 *Fig. 2*

TWILL for Army Shirts
FLANNEL for Fatigues
POCKETING for Uniforms
ABRASIVE CLOTH for Machines
SHEETS for Hospitals and Targets
CHAMBRAY for Navy Shirts
TOWELS for the Army
MARQUISETTE for Head Nets
BANDOLEER CLOTH for Bullets
BLANKETS for Merchant Ships
—*Pepperell Mill ad of 1942*

HAT

March 11, 1930

Morris Treiman

80,716

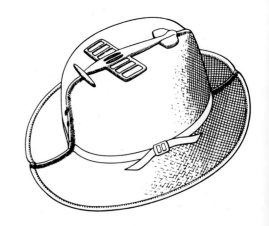

Albert, Allen D. *Official View Book: A Century of Progress Exposition*. Chicago: The Reuben H. Donnelly Corporation, 1933.

Andrews, J. J. C. *The Well-Built Elephant and Other Roadside Attractions: A Tribute to American Eccentricity*. New York: Congdon and Weed, Inc., 1984.

Annan, David. *Robot*. New York: Bounty Books, 1976.

Ant Farm, and Lord, Chip. *AutoAmerica: A Trip Down U.S. Highways from World War II to the Future*. New York: E. P. Dutton and Co., Inc., 1978.

Arnold, Schwinn & Co. *"For the Ride of a Lifetime!"* brochure for Schwinn Bicycles, 1941.

Arts Council of Great Britain. *Thirties: British Art and Design Before the War*. Arts Council of Great Britain, 1979.

Baeder, John. *Diners*. New York: Harry N. Abrams, Inc., 1978.

_____. *Gas, Food, and Lodging*. New York: Abbeville Press, 1982.

Bailey, Joseph A., and Lahue, Kalton C. *Glass, Brass, and Chrome: The American 35mm Miniature Camera*. Norman: University of Oklahoma Press, 1972.

Boissiere, Olivier. *Streamline: Le Design Americain Des Annees 30-40*. Paris: Editions Rivages, 1987.

Boyne, Walter J. *The Leading Edge*. New York: Stewart, Tabori and Chang, Inc., 1986.

_____. *Power Behind the Wheel: Creativity and Evolution of the Automobile*. New York: Stewart, Tabori and Chang, Inc., 1988.

Burke, Wallace R. "Evolution of the Unobviousness Standard, 35 USC 103, For Design Patents," paper for the National Conference on Industrial Design Law and Practice, University of Baltimore School of Law, 10-11 March, 1989.

Bush, Donald J. *The Streamlined Decade*. New York: George Braziller, Inc., 1975.

Collins, Philip. *Radios: The Golden Age*. San Francisco: Chronicle Books, 1987.

Coppersmith, Fred and Lynx, J. J. *Patents Applied for: A Century of Fantastic Inventions*. Co-ordination Press and Publicity Ltd., 1949.

Delear, Frank J. *Airplanes and Helicopters of the U.S. Navy*. New York: Dodd, Mead & Company, 1982.

Dreyfuss, Henry. *Designing for People*. New York: Simon and Schuster, 1955.

Drury, George H. *The Historical Guide to North American Railroads*. Milwaukee: Kalmbach Publishing Co., 1985.

Flat 4 Project. *Vintage Volkswagens*. San Francisco: Chronicle Books, 1985.

Forty, Adrian, *Objects of Desire: Design and Society from Wedgewood to IBM*. New York: Pantheon Books, 1986.

Frattolillo, Rinaldo, and Salmieri, Steve. *American Grilles*. New York: Harcourt Brace Jovanovich, 1979.

Friedel, Robert. *A Material World: An Exhibition at the National Museum of American History*. Washington: Smithsonian Institution, 1988.

Geier, Oscar A., and Richards, William Evarts. *Patents, Trademarks and Copyrights: Law and Practices*, 5th Edition. New York: 1930.

Georges, Rip, and Heiman, Jim. *California Crazy: Roadside Vernacular Architecture*. San Francisco: Chronicle Books, 1980.

Greif, Martin. *Depression Modern: The Thirties Style in America*. New York: Universe Books, 1975.

Gutman, Richard J. S., and Kaufman, Elliot. *American Diner*. New York: Harper and Row, Publishers, 1979.

Harrison, Helen A., curator. *Dawn of a New Day: The New York World's Fair 1939/1940*. New York: The Queens Museum, 1980.

Henkin, Bill, and Lynch, Vincent. *Jukebox: The Golden Age*. Berkeley: Lancaster-Miller, Inc., 1981.

Hennessey, William J. *Russel Wright: American Designer*. Cambridge: The MIT Press, 1983.

Heskett, John. *Industrial Design*. London: Thames and Hudson, Ltd., 1980.

Kinnaird, Clark, ed. *It Happened in 1945*. New York: Duell, Sloan and Pearce, 1946.

Kitahara, Teruhisa. CARS: *Tin Toy Dreams*. San Francisco: Chronicle Books, 1985.

Kostka, William J., ed. 1935. *Modern Mechanix & Inventions Magazine*, volume XIV, number 3 and 4.

Lindbergh, Charles A. *We*. New York: G. P. Putnam's Sons, 1927.

Loewy, Raymond. *Industrial Design*. Woodstock: The Overlook Press, 1979.

Mahoney, Tom, ed. 1936. *Modern Mechanix & Inventions Magazine*, volume XVI, number 4.

Morgan, Willard D. ed. 1941. *The Complete Photographer*, issue 9, volume 2.

Mott, Kelsey Martin, and Ringer, Barbara A. "Design Patents," *Encyclopedia of Patent Practice and Invention Management*, Calvert, Robert, ed. New York: Reinhold Publishing Co., 1964.

Nader, Ralph. *Unsafe at Any Speed*. New York: Pocket Books, 1966.

New York World's Fair Merchandising Department. *New York World's Fair Licensed Merchandise*. New York: New York World's Fair 1939 Inc., 1939.

Pilgrim, Dianne H.; Tashijan, Dickran; and Wilson, Richard Guy. *The Machine Age: 1918-1941*. New York: Harry N. Abrams, Inc., 1986.

Pulos, Arthur J. *American Design Ethic: A History of Industrial Design to 1940*. Cambridge: The MIT Press, 1983.

Richardson, Robert O. *How to Get Your Own Patent*. New York: Sterling Publishing Co., 1981.

Rosenberg, Manuel, ed. 1937. *The Advertiser*, volume 8, number 6.

Scherman, David E., ed. *Life Goes to War*. New York: Simon & Schuster, 1986.

Sexton, Richard. *American Style: Classic Product Design from Airstream to Zippo*. San Francisco: Chronicle Books, 1987.

Teague, Walter Dorwin. *Design This Day: The Technique of Order in the Machine Age*. New York: Harcourt, Brace & Co., 1940.

Time-Life Books, eds. *This Fabulous Century*, vols. 4, 5. New York: Time-Life Books, Inc., 1969.

Travelers New Bureau, eds. *Smash Hits of the Year: The Travelers 1940 Book of Street and Highway Accident Data*. Hartford: The Travelers Insurance Company, 1940.

United States Department of Commerce, Patent & Trademark Office. *The National Inventors Hall of Fame*. United States Department of Commerce, Patent & Trademark Office, 1989.

_____. *Manual of Patent Examining Procedure*. Section 1500, United States Department of Commerce, Patent & Trademark Office, 1986.

_____. *Guide for Design Patent Drawings*. United States Department of Commerce, Patent & Trademark Office, 1989.

_____. *Guide for Filing Design Patent Applications*. United States Department of Commerce, Patent & Trademark Office, 1989.

_____. *Guide for Patent Draftsmen*. United States Department of Commerce, Patent & Trademark Office, 1961.

_____. *General Information Concerning Patents*. United States Department of Commerce, Patent & Trademark Office, 1989.

_____. *The Story of the U.S. Patent and Trademark Office*. United States Department of Commerce, Patent & Trademark Office, 1988.

Vassos, John, and Ruth. *Contempo: This American Tempo*. New York: E. P. Dutton and Company, Inc., 1929.

Whalen, Grover. *A Trip to the New York World's Fair with Bobby and Betty*. New York: Dodge Publishing Company, 1938.

Wooldridge, E. T. *Winged Wonders: The Story of the Flying Wings*. Washington: Smithsonian Institution Press, 1983.